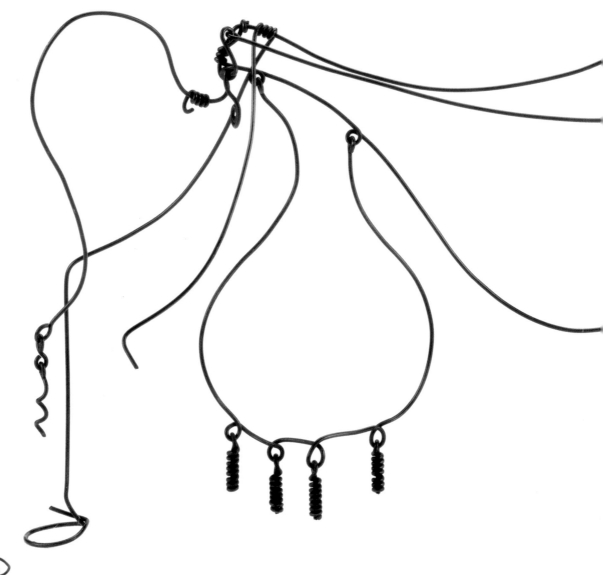

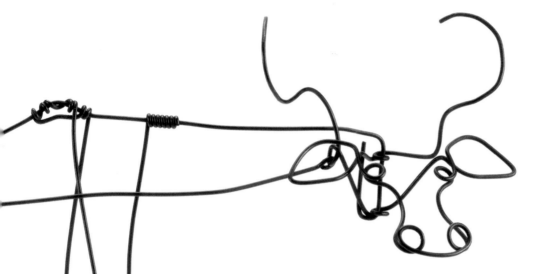

Please Be Seated

Recipes for Entertaining
from the
MUSEUM OF FINE ARTS, BOSTON

MFA PUBLICATIONS
a division of the Museum of Fine Arts, Boston

Library of Congress Control Number: 2002105901
ISBN: 0-87846-651-7

Published by MFA Publications
a division of the Museum of Fine Arts, Boston
465 Huntington Avenue
Boston, MA 02115
www.mfa-publications.org
Additional copies of this book may be ordered from
the Museum Shops, Museum of Fine Arts, Boston
(617) 369-3575
www.mfa.org/shop

Photographs of the works of art are from the
Museum of Fine Arts, Boston
Produced by the MFA Senior Associates of the
Museum of Fine Arts, Boston

Copyedited by Patricia Kiyono
Designed by John Hubbard
Typeset by Jennifer Sugden
Proofread by Sherri Schultz
Produced by Marquand Books, Inc., Seattle
Printed and bound by CS Graphics Pte., Ltd., Singapore

Photograph Credits: The works below are reproduced by permission of the artist and/or credited organization that represents the rights of the artist or the artist's estate:

Dale Broholm, Bench, 1986; Wendell Castle, Settee, 1979; Peter Dean, Side chairs, 1987; Thomas Hucker, Bench, 1982; John Lewis, *Glacier Bench*, 1997; Kristina Madsen, Side chair, 1989; Sam Maloof, Rocking chair, 1975; Judy Kensley McKie, Bench, 1979; Eric O'Leary, Bench, 1998; Robert Rauschenberg, *Plain Salt (Cardboards)*, 1971, © Robert Rauschenberg/Licensed by VAGA, New York, NY; Martin Simpson, *Three's Company*, 1994; Joyce Sisneros, *Pueblo Bread Bakers*, 1984; Jay Stanger, Chair, 1985; Photograph of the Mushrooms netsuke by Masami Sugimoto; Edward Weston, *Pepper*, 1930, by permission of The Lane Collection; Toots Zynsky, *Soleggiata Serena*, 2000

Front cover: Stuart Davis, *Apples and Jug*, 1923

Back cover: Thomas Rowlandson, *A Footman Spilling the Soup (Directions to Footmen)*

Front cover flap: Gujari Ragini, from an illustrated *Ragamala* manuscript, Northern India (Rajasthan, Mewar), about 1730

Back cover flap: Nicholas Lancret, *Luncheon Party in a Park (Déjeuner de jambon)*, about 1735

Page 1: Sideboard, 1850–60, made by Ignatius Lutz, 1817–1860

Pages 2–3: Alexander Calder, *Cow*, about 1926

Contents

7   Foreword

8   Ingredients, Methods, Equipment

18   Hors d'oeuvres, First Courses, Beverages

38   Soups, Stews, Chowders

52   Salads, Dressings, Seasonings

72   Breads, Rolls, Sandwiches

88   Seafood, Poultry, Meats

120   Casseroles, Pastas, Quiches

132   Vegetables, Grains, Condiments

156   Fruits, Custards, Sweets

181   List of Works of Art

186   Acknowledgments

189   Index

Bench, 1979
Made by JUDY KENSLEY MCKIE, born 1944

Foreword

It gives me great pleasure to introduce *Please Be Seated,* the newest publishing endeavor of the Ladies Committee Associates of the Museum of Fine Arts, Boston. Designed for entertaining at home, this cookbook contains more than one hundred seventy-five recipes contributed by curators, administrators, docents, other staff members, and volunteers. Because our Museum family represents multiple cultures, we bring you tastes from Boston that reflect the best of both New England and the world.

The title, *Please Be Seated,* is taken from an important initiative of our American Decorative Arts collection to acquire contemporary handcrafted chairs, settees, benches, and stools that provide comfortable seating throughout the Museum's collections. The concept underlying this program is to enable our visitors to experience, while viewing masterpieces in the galleries, works of the greatest craftsmen of our age.

The sixty-two works of art that accompany the recipes, however, are drawn from all departments within the Museum, reflecting the depth and breadth of our holdings. They illustrate the artistry associated with food as well as its celebratory nature. We hope this book will inspire you to experience the joy of informal and elegant entertaining with family and friends. Please be seated!

Malcolm Rogers
Ann and Graham Gund Director

Ingredients,
Methods,
Equipment

The pleasures of preparation are part of the fun of entertaining. *Please Be Seated* is filled with carefully chosen recipes and ideas that will inspire your creativity. You'll want to shop for the freshest ingredients to achieve both delicacy and depth of flavor. From sauté pan to colander, from meat thermometer to flour sifter, bring all the resources of your kitchen into your efforts. Your guests will reward you with smiles of satisfaction.

Bench, 1986
Made by DALE BROHOLM, born 1956

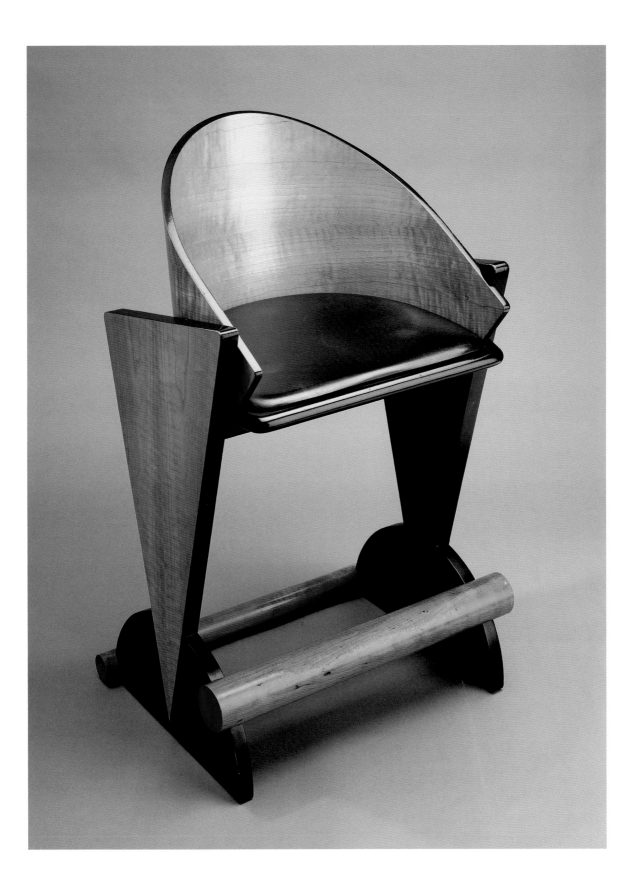

GUSTAVE CAILLEBOTTE, 1848–1894
Fruit Displayed on a Stand, about 1881–82

Ingredients

Successful cooking always starts with the freshest and finest ingredients. Beyond this general rule, the experienced cook makes a distinction between baking and other kinds of cooking. Because of the chemistry involved in baking, you should use the exact ingredients and amounts listed in a recipe. Even a small variation in measurement can change the balance of a recipe enough to cause a poor result. Other kinds of food preparation allow more flexibility, but keep in mind that the original recipe provides an authentic guide that has been tested for a balance of ingredients and flavors.

The following descriptions specify the particular ingredients you should look for as you prepare to cook. All ingredients should be at room temperature unless otherwise stated.

BAKING POWDER: Use fresh double-action baking powder that is aluminum free. Fresh baking powder will fizz when added to water.

BAKING SODA: Test that your baking soda is very fresh. Active baking soda will fizz when added to vinegar.

BUTTER: Recipes call for either butter (salted) or unsalted butter. Unsalted butter is richer in flavor because it contains a higher ratio of cream to water.

CHOCOLATE: Select a very high quality dark or white chocolate.

CHOCOLATE CHIPS: Always buy *premium-brand* chips. Use semisweet chocolate chips unless milk chocolate chips or white baking chips are specifically called for.

CITRUS FRUIT: Remove only the colored portion of the peel. The pith (white part underneath) tends to be bitter. Use only freshly squeezed juices.

COCOA: Purchase *Dutch processed,* unsweetened cocoa powder. Do not substitute prepared cocoa mix.

CRÈME FRAÎCHE: This slightly fermented dairy product falls between fresh and sour cream in texture and taste. It lends a tang to soups and sauces and works well as a topping for berries.

EGGS: Buy large, Grade A eggs, unless otherwise specified. The risk of salmonella from eggs is limited but real. You can reduce the risk by buying clean fresh eggs with flawless shells and refrigerating any prepared dishes that will not be consumed within an hour. For recipes in which the eggs will not be cooked, look for pasteurized eggs or take these precautions: Combine the yolks with the liquid called for in the recipe and stir over very low heat until the mixture registers 160 degrees or just begins to bubble; then plunge the bottom of the pan into cold water to cool the mix quickly. Combine the whites with the sugar called for in the recipe and beat over hot water until the whites stand in soft peaks.

FLOUR: Recipes call for white, all-purpose flour, a blend of hard and soft wheat flours. It may be either bleached or unbleached. On occasion, cake flour may be specified; it is a highly refined flour, milled from soft winter wheat. All flour has a tendency to pack on standing, so always sift flour once before measuring, even if the flour label says "presifted."

FRUITS: Dried fruits (apricots, dates, raisins, currants) must be soft and fresh because baking will not soften them. If they have become too dry, steam them over hot water for a few minutes until they plump; then dry them between layers of paper towels.

HERBS: Use fresh herbs whenever possible. If you must substitute dried for fresh, use the guide of 1 teaspoon dried for 1 tablespoon fresh and adjust the formula, as necessary, for variations among brands.

MEAT, POULTRY, AND SEAFOOD: Our suggested internal temperatures vary to achieve a desired taste or texture in particular recipes. The United States Department of Agriculture (USDA) recommends an internal temperature of at least 160 degrees for all meats to reduce the risk of illness caused by bacteria. Poultry should be cooked until the juices run clear, 175 to 180 degrees for a whole bird or dark meat and 160 to 165 degrees for the breasts or ground poultry. Fish should be cooked until just opaque and the flesh lightly flakes when tested with a fork.

MILK: Use *whole*, grade A milk.

NUTS: Use fresh nuts. A particular nut may be specified in a recipe but, generally speaking, pecans, walnuts, almonds, and hazelnuts are inter-changeable. Since nuts turn rancid fairly quickly, you should store them in the freezer.

OIL: Always choose the best quality available. *Olive* oils range from the first cold pressing (extra virgin) to additional, filtered pressings (refined, light). First pressings are usually more flavorful, while later pressings have a higher smoke point. *Vegetable* and some *seed* oils serve as inexpensive cooking and salad ingredients. *Nut* and some *seed* oils are highly flavored oils often used for dressings or for drizzling over foods; many have a fairly low smoke point and need refrigeration after opening.

PASTA: The variety of pasta shapes is extensive. Some lend themselves better than others to particular sauces. Compact shapes like penne (tubes), farfalle (bows), or fusilli (spirals) are best for entertaining. Long flat shapes, like spaghetti, linguine, or fettuccine, which require twirling, are better suited to informal family gatherings. Fresh pasta will cook in the time it takes for the water to return to a boil. Dry pasta will take longer, the cooking time varying according to its size and shape.

PEPPER: Use ground black pepper unless the recipe specifies white or cayenne. For freshly ground pepper, grind peppercorns with a good pepper mill.

SALT: Different salts affect the flavor of food differently. Oversalting is difficult to correct, so it is better to taste before increasing the amount, especially when doubling a recipe. *Table salt,* which is highly refined, is the most common choice for cooking and at the table. *Sea salt,* distilled from seawater, has a more distinctive flavor and should be used more sparingly. Fine sea salt can substitute for table salt because it dissolves instantly; coarse sea salt adds texture to foods. *Kosher salt,* also coarse, offers better control than table salt because the grains do not melt or penetrate the food and they thereby impart a less salty flavor.

SPICES: Measurements are for dried, ground spices unless otherwise noted.

SUGAR: Use white, fine granulated sugar. If brown sugar is called for, the recipe will specify light or dark. Confectioners' sugar is 10-X powdered sugar; it should be sifted before measuring or decorating.

VANILLA: Purchase only pure vanilla extract packaged in dark glass bottles. Imitation vanilla contains synthetic vanillin made from wood pulp by-products and not from vanilla beans.

VINEGAR: Always use the best quality available. *Cider* vinegar is an all-purpose fruit vinegar made from fermented apples. *Rice* vinegar, which has a delicate flavor and lower acidity, is most often used in Asian recipes. *Wine* vinegar is produced from either red or white wine and fermented in oak casks. *Distilled white* vinegar is made from grain and is often used for pickling. *Balsamic* vinegar is a boiled wine vinegar with added caramel; the very highest quality, unique to Modena, Italy, is sweet yet pungent, aged in barrels for ten years, and used by drops or teaspoonfuls.

WASABI: Wasabi, a fiery green Japanese horseradish, is available in ready-to-use tubes of paste or small tins of powder found in the international foods sections of some supermarkets and in Asian food stores. You can easily reconstitute the powder by adding a small amount of warm water and mixing until a smooth, thick paste is formed. Start with 1 part powder to 4 parts water. Adjust the powder or water according to your taste. Let it sit, covered, for 10 minutes to allow its flavor to mature. Powdered wasabi will keep indefinitely, but once mixed, it should be used the same day. Paste in opened tubes keeps for a year refrigerated. Fresh wasabi is light green, nubby, and about 3 to 5 inches long. Grate only as much as you will use.

JEAN FRANCOIS MILLET, 1814–1875
Young Woman Churning Butter, about 1848–51

Methods

Preparation

DEVEIN: Remove the dark vein down the back of the tail of a lobster or shrimp.

DICE: Cut into pieces of equal size, approximately ⅛ to ¼ inch.

DREDGE: Coat all surfaces lightly with flour, sugar, or another substance such as bread crumbs.

JULIENNE: Cut food, most often vegetables, into thin strips of equal length.

MARINATE: Soak in a liquid mixture that usually has a vinegar or wine base and is seasoned with herbs and spices.

MINCE: Cut into fine pieces.

PURÉE: Press through a fine sieve or food mill, or process in a blender or food processor to a smooth, thick mixture.

TOAST: Lightly brown ingredients. Nuts and seeds can be toasted in an ungreased pan in a preheated 350-degree oven or stirred in a dry skillet over low heat until desired browning is achieved.

Mixing

BEAT: With an electric mixer at high speed, briskly blend ingredients over and over to enclose air and make the mixture light. By hand, use a vertical circular motion.

BLEND OR MIX: Combine two or more ingredients so that each loses its identity.

CREAM: Beat softened butter with an electric mixer or a wooden spoon until smooth and fluffy. Gradually add sugar and continue mixing until substance is light.

FOLD: Combine two prepared mixtures, the lighter on top of the heavier. Use a spatula to cut gently through the center of mixtures; lightly lift and fold over ingredients. Repeat carefully until blended. Do not overmix.

KNEAD: Bring dough to a uniform, elastic mixture by pressing, turning, and folding by hand, with the dough hook of an electric mixer, or in a food processor.

STIR: With an electric mixer on medium-low speed, mix until all ingredients are just blended. By hand, holding a spoon upright, use a horizontal circular motion.

WHIP: Beat light mixtures, such as egg whites and creams, at the highest mixer speed.

WHISK: Beat with a wire whisk until blended and smooth.

Cooking

AL DENTE: Cooked until just tender or firm to the bite; usually refers to vegetables and pasta.

BAKE: Cook in an oven, preheated to a specific temperature.

BASTE: Brush or spoon a liquid over food during cooking to keep the surface moist and add flavor.

BOIL: Heat liquid until bubbles break the surface, or cook food in boiling liquid.

BROIL: Cook on a rack under direct heat, such as in the broiler of an electric or gas oven.

CARAMELIZE: Melt sugar over low heat, without burning, until golden to dark brown, or cook onions in butter over low heat, without burning, until golden to dark brown.

DEGLAZE: Quickly reduce sauce by adding a small amount of water, wine, vinegar, or other liquid to the pan after sautéing meat or other food; stir to gather up the browned pieces and simmer until the sauce reaches the desired consistency.

GRILL: Cook on a rack over direct heat, such as on a gas or charcoal grill.

MELT: Liquefy an ingredient over low heat or boiling water, or in a microwave.

POACH: Cook food, usually uncovered, at a temperature where the surface of the liquid barely moves.

PREHEAT: Set oven at temperature specified by the recipe and preheat for 15 minutes. *If using a glass pan,* set oven 25 degrees lower than temperature recommended in recipe.

REDUCE: Cook a liquid, sauce, or stock over high heat to decrease its amount and intensify its flavor.

ROAST: Cook meat or vegetables uncovered, without additional liquid, in an oven.

SAUTÉ: Cook quickly, while stirring, over moderately high heat in a small amount of fat.

SCALD: Heat a liquid just until small bubbles form at the edges of the pan.

SEAR: Brown the surface of meat or other food quickly over high heat to seal in juices.

SIMMER: Cook a liquid or cook food in a liquid just below the boiling point.

STIR-FRY: Fry very quickly over high heat while stirring continuously.

Equipment

Use standard measuring cups and spoons that conform to United States Bureau of Standards specifications. Unless otherwise stated in a recipe, all measurements are level.

For liquid measures, use a glass cup marked on the side and having a top that extends above the cup line (to prevent spilling). For accuracy, set the cup on a level surface, pour liquid into it, and check the exact amount at eye level.

To measure dry ingredients, use nested metal cups available in sets of four (1 cup, ½ cup, ⅓ cup, ¼ cup). These do not have extensions above the cup measure, nor do they have lips. For a level measurement, sift or lightly spoon dry ingredients into the cup, and draw a straight metal spatula across the top. The only exception to this rule is brown sugar; it must be packed into the cup so firmly that it holds the shape of the cup when turned out.

The standard set of measuring spoons includes 1 tablespoon, 1 teaspoon, ½ teaspoon, and ¼ teaspoon. Fill the spoon to level for liquid ingredients. For dry ingredients, fill the spoon to heaping and level off with a straight metal spatula.

BLENDER: An electric tool, either a standing model or hand-held immersion style, used to combine ingredients thoroughly into a creamy, soupy mixture or liquid.

DUTCH OVEN: A 6- to 8-quart sturdy pot with a tightly fitted lid; used on stove top.

FOOD PROCESSOR: An electric tool used to grate, grind, chop, slice, or purée large amounts of food quickly.

MIXER: An electric tool, standing or hand-held model, used to combine ingredients at various speeds.

NONREACTIVE MATERIALS: Stainless steel, glass, or enamel pans, which do not react chemically with acidic foods and beverages. (Aluminum and copper are two metals that react with such foods as tomatoes.)

Note: Italicized comments throughout the book provide tips on preparation and presentation that will give your dishes a special flair.

Hors d'oeuvres, First Courses, Beverages

Before anyone is seated, you can delight the eye and satisfy hunger pangs with a selection of hors d'oeuvres arranged attractively on a lovely tray. Perhaps after a festive beverage, you'll begin the meal with a delicious first course. Whether you choose gleaming silver and sparkling crystal or charming ceramic serving pieces to highlight the presentation of your food, bring out your best!

Bench, 1982
Made by THOMAS HUCKER, born 1955

Hors d'oeuvres

Artichoke Cheesecake

Dry bread crumbs
1 (6-ounce) jar marinated
    artichoke hearts
24 ounces cream cheese,
    softened
5 ounces (1¼ cups) feta,
    crumbled
2 garlic cloves, minced
1½ teaspoons oregano,
    minced
3 eggs
¼ cup chopped scallions
1 teaspoon chopped pimiento

Grease a 9-inch springform pan and sprinkle it lightly with bread crumbs. Drain artichokes, reserving 2 tablespoons of the marinade, and chop. Combine cream cheese, feta, garlic, and oregano in a large bowl and beat until smooth. Beat in the eggs just until well mixed. Stir in artichokes, scallions, pimiento, and reserved marinade. Spoon mixture into the pan and cover loosely with foil. Bake in a preheated 325-degree oven for 40 to 45 minutes, or until the edge is firm but the center still appears slightly soft when the pan is shaken. Cool on a wire rack and then chill, covered, for 2 to 24 hours. Remove the side of the pan and garnish with pimiento, fresh herbs, or seasonal decorations. Serve slightly chilled or at room temperature with crackers or toasted baguette slices.

YIELD: 16 SERVINGS

Chiles and Cheese

2 (4½-ounce) cans chopped
    green chiles (medium hot)
10 ounces sharp Cheddar
3 eggs
3 tablespoons milk
Large tortilla chips or crackers

Butter an 8-inch quiche dish. Spread chiles over the bottom of the dish. Grate cheese and sprinkle evenly over chiles. Beat eggs and milk together and pour over all. Bake in a preheated 350-degree oven for 30 minutes, or until lightly brown. Serve warm with tortilla chips or crackers.

YIELD: 10 TO 12 SERVINGS

UNIDENTIFIED ARTIST
Persian, Timurid painting, 1425–50,
mounted in an album, 1544–45
Prince and Lady under Flowering Branch, page from
an album made for Prince Behrain Mirza

Sweet Pea Guacamole

2 tablespoons extra virgin
  olive oil
2 tablespoons lime juice
¼ bunch cilantro or parsley,
  trimmed of long stems
1 jalapeño pepper, seeded
1 (1-pound) bag frozen baby
  sweet peas, thawed
¾ teaspoon salt
¼ teaspoon cumin
¼ medium red onion, finely
  diced
Tortilla chips, pita wedges,
  or crudités

Combine oil, lime juice, cilantro, and jalapeño in a blender or food processor until cilantro and pepper are roughly puréed. Add peas, salt, and cumin and blend just until smooth; the lumps that remain add textural interest. Scrape into a bowl and mix in onion. Serve with tortilla chips, pita, or crudités.

YIELD: 2 CUPS

Use more jalapeño and cilantro for a spicier dip. Unlike guacamole made with avocado, this dip retains its color. It can be made a day ahead, covered, and refrigerated. For a colorful presentation, serve in two hollow red bell peppers.

Marinated Mushrooms

2 pounds medium whole
  mushrooms, stems removed
1 cup butter
2 cups burgundy
1 cup boiling water
1 beef bouillon cube
1 tablespoon Worcestershire
  sauce
½ teaspoon pepper
½ teaspoon garlic powder
½ teaspoon dried dill

Clean mushrooms with a damp cloth or, if crevices are very dirty, rinse lightly under cold water, taking care that mushrooms do not absorb moisture; pat dry. Combine all ingredients in a large pot. Bring to a slow boil on medium heat. Reduce to simmer and cook 5 to 6 hours, covered. Remove the cover and simmer slowly for another 2 to 3 hours, until liquid barely covers mushrooms. Refrigerate until ready to serve. Reheat and serve in a hot chafing dish.

YIELD: 12 SERVINGS

Chicken Chutney Canapés

¼ cup chutney, drained and minced

¼ cup unsalted butter, softened

3 tablespoons minced scallions

1 tablespoon Dijon mustard

8 slices thinly sliced, dense whole grain bread, crusts removed

1 large (6-ounce) boneless, skinless chicken breast, poached and thinly sliced

Cilantro leaves

16 seedless green grapes, halved

In a small bowl, combine chutney, butter, scallions, and mustard and mix until well blended. Spread bread with three-quarters of the chutney mixture and cut each slice into quarters. Trim the chicken into squares to fit the bread and place on canapés. Garnish with a cilantro leaf, a dot of the remaining chutney mixture, and a grape half.

YIELD: 32 CANAPÉS

LUIS MELÉNDEZ, 1716–1780
Still Life with Bread, Ham, Cheese, and Vegetables, about 1770

Chicken Liver Pâté

¾ cup butter, divided
2 medium onions, chopped
   (about 2 cups)
1 clove garlic, chopped
1 pound chicken livers
1 teaspoon flour
1 teaspoon salt
½ teaspoon dried thyme leaves
¼ teaspoon sugar
¼ teaspoon pepper
¼ teaspoon dried oregano
1 bay leaf
⅓ cup currants
2 tablespoons brandy or
   bourbon
Chopped parsley (optional)
1 egg, hard-cooked and finely
   sieved (optional)
Melba rounds

Melt half the butter in a skillet and sauté onions and garlic over medium-high heat about 5 minutes, or until softened but not brown. Add remaining butter and chicken livers. Cook 5 to 10 minutes over medium heat, stirring occasionally, until livers are no longer pink. Sprinkle with flour and add salt, thyme, sugar, pepper, oregano, and bay leaf. Cover and simmer for 1 minute. Remove from the heat and discard bay leaf. Purée mixture in a blender or food processor. Add currants and spirits. Chill or serve at room temperature. Garnish with parsley or grated egg and serve with Melba rounds.

YIELD: 2½ CUPS *The pâté can be refrigerated for 2 days.*

Smoked Salmon Toasts

½ pound smoked salmon, cut
   into small pieces
1 tablespoon chopped red
   onion
2 ribs celery, minced
2 tablespoons small capers
Freshly ground pepper, to taste
16 bread rounds, thinly sliced
   and lightly toasted, or water
   crackers

Combine salmon, onion, celery, capers, and pepper and mound onto bread rounds or crackers.

VARIATION: Bind mixture with 2 tablespoons sour cream, 1 teaspoon horseradish, and ½ teaspoon lemon juice.

YIELD: 16 CANAPÉS *May also be served with endive or as a filling for baked potatoes, pastry cups, or omelets.*

Summer Shrimp Salsa

2 large tomatoes, peeled, seeded, and diced

½ red bell pepper, seeded and diced

½ yellow bell pepper, seeded and diced

1 jalapeño pepper, seeded and diced

½ English cucumber, diced

½ cup fresh or frozen corn kernels, uncooked

2 tablespoons chopped parsley

2 tablespoons chopped cilantro

2 tablespoons lime juice

1½ teaspoons salt

½ teaspoon pepper

1 ripe avocado, diced

½ pound shrimp, cooked, shelled, and diced

Cilantro leaves

Tortilla chips or toasted pita wedges

Combine tomatoes, peppers, cucumber, corn, parsley, cilantro, lime juice, salt, and pepper in a large serving bowl. Just before serving, add avocado and shrimp. Garnish with additional cilantro leaves. Serve with tortilla chips or pita wedges.

YIELD: 4 CUPS

For a different presentation, substitute endive or crudités for the chips. Another alternative is to serve the shrimp and salsa separately.

Provençal Tartlets

3 tablespoons extra virgin
   olive oil
I cup julienned red bell pepper
I cup julienned yellow bell
   pepper
I cup thinly sliced red onion
½ teaspoon *herbes de Provence*
Salt, to taste
Freshly ground black pepper,
   to taste
I large clove garlic, minced
Butter-flavored cooking spray
18 to 20 wonton wrappers,
   2½ inches square
4 ounces goat cheese
¼ cup heavy cream
¼ teaspoon white pepper

Heat olive oil in a small saucepan over low heat. Add peppers, onion, *herbes de Provence,* salt, and black pepper and cook, covered, over low heat for about 30 minutes. Uncover, add garlic, and continue cooking for about 10 minutes. Remove from the heat and set aside to cool. Drain the oil that separates from the peppers. Spray a nonstick mini muffin pan with cooking spray. Press wrappers into each mold to form cups and spray lightly again. Bake in a preheated 325-degree oven for 7 to 10 minutes, or until light brown. Remove cups from the pan and set aside to cool. Reduce the oven temperature to 250 degrees. In a small bowl, combine goat cheese with half the cream; add white pepper. Stir in as much remaining cream as necessary, a little at a time, until the mixture is smooth. Place about ½ teaspoon of goat cheese mixture into each cup, using enough to cover the base. Top with a teaspoon of the pepper mixture. Place tartlets on a baking sheet and bake for 10 minutes, or until warmed through. Serve immediately.

YIELD: 18 TO 20 TARTLETS

Shells can be made ahead; after baking, cool completely and store in an airtight container until ready for use.

Eggplant Crostini

2 firm eggplants, unpeeled
Cooking spray
1 teaspoon dried oregano
1 teaspoon red pepper flakes
1 clove garlic, minced
1 tablespoon capers
A few basil leaves, chopped
¼ cup balsamic vinegar
½ cup extra virgin olive oil
1 (4-ounce) log goat cheese,
    room temperature
Baguette, sliced and toasted
    for crostini
Basil leaves or parsley

Cut eggplant crosswise into approximately ½-inch-thick slices. Place on a foil-lined broiler pan, spray lightly with olive oil, and broil on both sides until brown. Mix together oregano, red pepper flakes, garlic, capers, and basil. Place a single layer of eggplant in an earthenware baking dish. Sprinkle with some of the herb mixture and some of the vinegar and olive oil. Continue layering eggplant, herbs, and oil and vinegar until all eggplant slices are used. Let marinate approximately 1½ hours and then chop coarsely. To serve, thinly spread goat cheese on crostini slices and top with eggplant mixture. Garnish with basil leaves or parsley.

YIELD: 1¾ CUPS

Marinated Shrimp

1½ pounds shrimp, cooked,
    shelled, and deveined
¼ cup white vinegar
½ cup extra virgin olive oil
Kosher salt, to taste
Tabasco sauce, to taste
1 clove garlic, minced
2 tablespoons chopped parsley
2 tablespoons chopped scallions
2 tablespoons chopped dill
    pickle
Additional scallions for garnish
    (optional)

Prepare shrimp and set aside. Mix together remaining ingredients except additional scallions in a leakproof storage container and shake well. Add shrimp and refrigerate for 6 hours or overnight. Remove shrimp from marinade, arrange on a platter, garnish with additional thinly sliced scallions, if desired, and serve at room temperature with cocktail picks.

YIELD: 8 SERVINGS

Spicy Mussels

2 pounds mussels

5 small scallions, divided

1 cup sake

2 (⅛-inch) slices fresh ginger

1½ teaspoons minced garlic

½ to 1 tablespoon seeded,
    minced jalapeño pepper

1 tablespoon extra virgin
    olive oil

1 tablespoon rice vinegar

¾ teaspoon sesame oil

¼ teaspoon hot chili oil,
    or to taste

Salt, to taste

Scrub and debeard mussels. Cut 2 scallions into 2-inch pieces and place in a large saucepan with mussels, sake, and ginger. Cover and bring to a boil over high heat. Boil just until mussels have opened. Uncover and set aside to let mussels cool in the liquid. Remove mussels from liquid with a slotted spoon. Twist off and discard one side of each shell. Transfer mussels on the half shell to a serving platter. Cover tightly and refrigerate. Bring the cooking liquid to a boil and reduce to ½ cup, about 10 minutes. Strain into a small bowl, discarding ginger and scallions. (The recipe can be prepared to this point up to one day ahead; cover and refrigerate mussels and liquid separately.) Before serving, sauté garlic and jalapeño in olive oil. Combine with mussel liquid, vinegar, and oils. Spoon sauce over mussels, salt to taste, and garnish with remaining 3 scallions, thinly sliced.

YIELD: ABOUT 3 DOZEN

PIETER CLAESZ., 1597/1598–1661
Still Life with Wine Goblet and Oysters, 1630s

First Courses

Caramelized Onion Quesadillas

1 tablespoon extra virgin
    olive oil
1 large red onion, halved and
    thinly sliced crosswise
4 scallions, sliced
3 cloves garlic, minced
¾ teaspoon cumin
¼ teaspoon dried oregano
1 tablespoon lime juice
4 large (10-inch) flour tortillas
1 cup shredded jalapeño-Jack
1 cup shredded sharp Cheddar
Salsa
Sour cream

Heat oil in a skillet over medium-low heat. Add red onion, scallions, and garlic; cook, covered, stirring occasionally, until softened, about 15 minutes. Uncover and continue cooking until onions begin to turn golden. Add cumin and oregano; cook for 1 minute. Remove from heat and stir in lime juice. Place 2 tortillas side by side on an *ungreased* baking sheet. Divide onion mixture equally between tortillas and spread evenly; sprinkle with cheeses. Top with remaining tortillas. Bake in a preheated 400-degree oven for 8 to 10 minutes, or until heated through and tortillas are golden around the edges. Let stand 5 minutes. Cut each into eighths, and serve with salsa and sour cream.

YIELD: 4 SERVINGS

Marinated Mussels

4 pounds mussels
1 bay leaf
1 cup water
1 cup white wine

VINAIGRETTE
¾ cup extra virgin olive oil
¼ cup white wine vinegar
¼ cup minced scallions
¼ cup minced parsley
1 teaspoon garlic salt
Salt, to taste
Pepper, to taste

Scrub and debeard mussels; place in a large pan with bay leaf, water, and wine. Cover and steam over low heat until mussels open, about 10 minutes; set aside to cool. Remove from shells, reserving half the shells for serving. To make vinaigrette, mix all ingredients until well blended. Marinate mussels in vinaigrette for 2 to 3 hours or overnight. Drain and serve ice cold on the half shell, topped with wasabi mayonnaise (page 68) or your favorite mustard sauce.

YIELD: 12 TO 16 SERVINGS

Salmon Crab Cakes

2 large red bell peppers

3 scallions, chopped and divided

5 tablespoons extra virgin olive oil, divided

2 tablespoons red wine vinegar

I egg, lightly beaten

I tablespoon Dijon mustard

½ cup cooked mashed potato

½ pound fresh salmon, cut into small pieces

½ pound fresh crabmeat

About 2 cups Fresh Bread Crumbs (page 144)

Char peppers in a roasting pan under a preheated broiler, turning occasionally until peppers have blackened on all sides and collapsed, about 10 to 20 minutes. Place them in a paper bag for 10 minutes to steam. Let cool; then peel, seed, and chop. In a small pan over medium heat, soften half the scallions in 3 tablespoons oil. Let cool, place with the oil in a food processor, and pulse with peppers and vinegar. Set this purée aside. In a large bowl, mix egg, mustard, potato, and remaining scallions and then stir in salmon and crab. Gradually add just enough bread crumbs (about I cup) to hold the mixture together. Shape into 8 cakes. Spread the remaining crumbs on a plate and press into both sides of the patties. In a large pan over medium-low heat, sauté the cakes in the remaining oil for about 8 minutes, turning once, until golden. Drain on paper towels and keep warm. Serve with red pepper purée.

YIELD: 8 FIRST-COURSE SERVINGS OR
4 LUNCHEON-SIZE SERVINGS

Purée can be made a day ahead. Serve with mixed greens lightly dressed with vinaigrette.

WEI JIUDING, active about 1350–1370
River Crab

Eggplant with Parmesan Curls

3 medium onions, chopped

3 cloves garlic, minced

5 tablespoons extra virgin olive oil, divided

1 large eggplant, cubed

4 cups canned tomatoes, cut up and liquid reserved

1 large green bell pepper, cut in strips

2 teaspoons sugar

1 tablespoon chopped basil

1½ tablespoons anchovy paste

½ cup chopped parsley

1 (2¼-ounce) can sliced ripe olives

1 (2¼-ounce) jar sliced pimientos

Salt, to taste

Pepper, to taste

Mixed greens

Parmesan curls

Using a large stockpot, sauté onions and garlic in 2 tablespoons oil until onions are transparent; remove with a slotted spoon and set aside. Add remaining oil, lower heat, and cook eggplant until very soft and slightly brown, about 25 minutes. Return onion and garlic to pot; add tomatoes with their liquid, pepper strips, sugar, basil, and anchovy paste. Cover and simmer 15 minutes. Add parsley, olives, and pimientos. Simmer, uncovered, stirring until mixture is thick, about 15 minutes. Add salt and pepper. Cool and refrigerate in a tightly covered container. Remove from refrigerator ½ hour before serving; place mixture on a bed of greens and garnish with Parmesan curls.

YIELD: 6 SERVINGS

It is best to make the eggplant mixture a day or two ahead so that flavors have time to blend. Use a vegetable peeler to make attractive cheese curls.

More First-Course Options

Expand your menu planning options by serving as a first course any soup or small portions of these items:

- Scallops in Wine (page 92)
- Smoked Salmon and Spinach Risotto (page 125)
- Chinese Chili Shrimp (page 93) and Roasted Asparagus (page 136)
- Roasted Red Peppers with Walnuts (page 137)
- Baked Semolina Gnocchi and Field Greens (page 145)

FRANS SNYDERS, 1579–1657
Vegetables and a Basket of Fruit on a Table

Beverages

Rhubarb Punch

3 cups fresh or frozen rhubarb,
   cut into ½-inch pieces
3 cups water
1 (6-ounce) can frozen pink
   lemonade
¾ cup sugar (or ½ cup honey)
1 (16-ounce) bottle ginger ale

In a large saucepan, combine rhubarb, water, lemonade, and sugar and bring to a boil; reduce heat and simmer 5 minutes, or until rhubarb is tender. Strain to remove pulp and chill remaining syrup. Just before serving, pour syrup over ice cubes in a pitcher or punch bowl and add ginger ale.

YIELD: 8 SERVINGS

Punch bowl and ladle, about 1885
Manufactured by the Gorham Manufacturing
Company, active 1865–1961

London Mimosa

¼ cup orange juice
I teaspoon grenadine
½ cup champagne

Pour juice and grenadine into a large crystal stemmed glass and add champagne. Serve chilled.

YIELD: 1 SERVING

This English version of the mimosa was invented at a London club in the early 1920s. Originally known as Buck's Fizz, this delightful beverage is an excellent way to use opened champagne.

Passion Fruit Punch

I bottle (750 ml) dry sparkling wine, chilled
½ cup passion fruit juice, chilled
½ cup cranberry juice, chilled
I lime, thinly sliced

Combine wine and juices in a punch bowl. Float lime wheels in the bowl and serve.

YIELD: 6 SERVINGS

Passion fruit juice can be found in specialty markets or in the international foods section of most large supermarkets.

Holiday Hot Mulled Punch

I cup sugar
½ cup water
2 cinnamon sticks
½ lemon, sliced
24 whole cloves
4 cups orange-grapefruit juice, heated
I quart claret
Brandy, to taste

Boil sugar, water, cinnamon, lemon slices, and cloves for 5 to 10 minutes to make a syrup. Add juice, claret, and brandy. Serve hot.

YIELD: 7 TO 8 SERVINGS

Fire Punch

1 bottle dry red wine
¾ cup sugar
3 whole cloves
¾ cup orange juice
¼ cup lemon juice
3 (1-inch) strips orange peel
2 (1-inch) strips lemon peel
½ cup sugar cubes
¼ cup rum, heated
Orange slices studded with
  whole cloves

Heat wine with sugar, cloves, juices, and peels. Do not boil. Pour into a flameproof, warmed punch bowl. Soak sugar cubes in rum, place them in a strainer over punch, and ignite. As cubes flame, gradually spoon remaining rum over cubes. When all sugar has melted into the punch, garnish with orange slices and ladle hot punch into cups.

YIELD: 8 SERVINGS

Egg Nog

5 eggs, separated
½ cup sugar
1 cup whiskey
1 cup rum
2 quarts milk
1 cup heavy cream

In a very large bowl, beat yolks with sugar until lemon colored. Stir in whiskey and rum. Add milk. In another bowl, whip egg whites until soft peaks form; fold into milk mixture. Whip heavy cream until soft peaks form and fold in. Beat to incorporate all ingredients.

YIELD: 15 TO 20 SERVINGS

This makes a very frothy beverage. When serving from a punch bowl, use your ladle to recombine the froth with the liquid before ladling into cups; if serving from a covered container, shake well to combine before pouring.

The Luncheon (from the series *La Noble Pastorale* or *Les Beaux Pastorales*)
Tapestry, France (Beauvais), 1756

Soups, Stews, Chowders

Steam rising from a shiny copper pot on the stove or a china tureen on the table signals warm nourishment for body and soul. Early settlers in New England combined the bounty of the sea and vegetables from their gardens with milk from their cows to make hearty meals. These stews and chowders offer sustenance and comfort as a main dish, while lighter soups can whet the appetite for the courses that will follow.

Three's Company, 1994
Made by MARTIN SIMPSON, born 1964

Soups

"One of Each" Soup

1 pint chicken stock
1 cup sliced banana
1 cup peeled, cubed white
    potato
1 cup chopped celery, tender
    inside ribs and leaves
1 cup peeled, cored, chopped
    apple
1 pint light cream
1 tablespoon curry powder

In a large uncovered saucepan, simmer chicken stock, banana, potato, celery, and apple until ingredients are tender, about 10 minutes. Transfer to a food processor or blender and blend until smooth. Stir in cream and curry when reheating.

YIELD: 4 SERVINGS

Make a day ahead, so that flavors will blend, and serve cold or hot. For a special presentation, float banana chips on top.

Cold Senegalese Soup

1 pound boneless, skinless
    chicken breast
3 cups chicken stock, divided
2 small onions, chopped
2 tablespoons extra virgin
    olive oil or butter
2 tablespoons curry powder
1 apple, peeled and chopped
Salt, to taste
Pepper, to taste
⅓ cup mango chutney
16 ounces plain yogurt

In a small saucepan, poach chicken in 1½ cups chicken stock for about 10 minutes. Meanwhile, sauté onions in a skillet with oil or butter, just until softened. Sprinkle with curry powder, stir, and continue to cook, stirring occasionally, for 3 to 4 minutes; add apple to pan. Drain poaching liquid from chicken into the apple/onion mixture. Add salt and pepper and let the apples and onions simmer. Cut chicken into chunks, put in a food processor with the chutney, and process until smooth. Pour the contents of the sauté pan into the food processor and purée the mixture. Pour into a large mixing bowl. Add yogurt and remaining 1½ cups chicken stock to the processor and pulse briefly. Whisk yogurt into chicken and chill.

YIELD: ABOUT 2 QUARTS

Wild Rice Soup

2 tablespoons butter
¼ cup chopped onion
¼ cup thinly sliced celery
¼ cup thinly sliced carrots
¼ cup chopped green bell
  pepper
1 tablespoon chopped
  pimientos
⅔ cup uncooked wild rice,
  rinsed and drained
4 cups chicken stock
2 cubes chicken bouillon
½ cup butter
¼ cup flour
2 cups milk

Melt butter in a 3-quart saucepan. Sauté onion, celery, carrots, and pepper until slightly soft; add pimientos. Rinse wild rice and add to vegetables. Add stock and bouillon, bring to a boil, cover, and simmer about 1 hour, until rice is tender and has expanded. Thin with water if needed. In a separate saucepan, melt butter, add flour, and stir over low heat until cooked and bubbly. Whisk in milk and continue stirring until thickened. Add resulting white sauce to soup and simmer for an additional 15 to 20 minutes.

YIELD: 4 SERVINGS

Wild rice, an unusual grain prized by early Native Americans as a special gift, grows in the clear lakes and streams of North America. This soup can be made ahead and frozen.

Curried Zucchini Soup

1 pound young zucchini, sliced
2 tablespoons minced onion
1 clove garlic, minced
2 tablespoons butter
¾ teaspoon curry powder
Salt, to taste
Pepper, to taste
1¾ cups chicken stock
½ cup light cream
Croutons or chopped chives

In a large covered saucepan over medium heat, cook zucchini, onion, and garlic in butter for 15 to 20 minutes, or until tender. Add curry powder, salt, and pepper. Spoon mixture into a food processor or blender; add stock and cream. Blend well and serve hot or cold with croutons or chopped chives.

YIELD: 4 SERVINGS

Simple and easy and a good soup base for broccoli or other vegetables. Curry powder makes this somewhat standard recipe unusual.

Soup tureen
England (Chelsea Factory), about 1755

Pear and Leek Bisque

5 large leeks
¼ cup butter
½ cup instant mashed potato
 flakes
2 (14½-ounce) cans pears,
 with liquid
I teaspoon dried thyme leaves
1½ teaspoons dried parsley
I bay leaf
6 cups chicken stock
I cup heavy cream
½ cup crumbled blue cheese
½ cup coarsely chopped
 pecans, toasted

Cut green leaves off leeks, split, rinse thoroughly, and thinly slice crosswise. In a large saucepan, sauté leeks in butter until golden brown. Add potato, pears, thyme, parsley, bay leaf, and stock and simmer about 15 minutes. Remove from heat, cool slightly, discard bay leaf, and stir in cream. Transfer to a food processor or blender and blend until smooth. Reheat over medium heat, stirring constantly. To garnish, lightly sprinkle each serving with blue cheese and pecans.

YIELD: 8 SERVINGS

Serve hot or cold, depending on the season, for two very different tastes.

White Gazpacho

2 English cucumbers, peeled
 and seeded
I medium clove garlic
1¼ cups chicken stock
1¼ cups sour cream
2 teaspoons rice vinegar
I teaspoon salt
¼ cup peeled, seeded,
 and diced tomato
¼ cup minced chives

Cut cucumbers into 2-inch chunks. Place cucumber and garlic in food processor or blender and blend until evenly puréed. (If using a blender, add some stock before puréeing.) Add chicken stock, sour cream, vinegar, and salt. Mix briefly, just to blend. Chill at least I hour. Serve soup in chilled glass bowls; garnish with diced tomato and chives.

VARIATION: Add ¼ cup chopped cilantro and 2 tablespoons lime juice.

YIELD: 4 SERVINGS

Grilled Vegetable Gazpacho

I medium eggplant, sliced
    lengthwise ½ inch thick
Salt
I red bell pepper, halved
    and seeded
I green bell pepper, halved
    and seeded
2 red onions, root intact
    and bulb quartered
I zucchini, sliced lengthwise
    ½ inch thick
I summer squash, sliced
    lengthwise ½ inch thick
I leek, halved lengthwise and
    thoroughly rinsed
2 ears corn
3 hot peppers, cored, seeded,
    and finely chopped
2 cloves garlic, crushed
Juice of 2 limes
¾ cup red wine vinegar
2 quarts tomato juice
I cup clam juice
⅛ teaspoon cumin
3 tablespoons chopped cilantro
I tablespoon sugar
Salt, to taste
Pepper, to taste
Cornbread croutons
Diced avocado

Sprinkle eggplant with salt and drain in a colander for 30 minutes; meanwhile, light the grill. Rinse eggplant and pat dry. Grill eggplant, bell peppers (skin side down), onions, zucchini, squash, leek, and corn until they are lightly charred and cooked through. When vegetables are cool enough to handle, peel bell peppers and chop coarsely; trim roots from onions. Coarsely chop the remaining grilled vegetables, remove corn kernels from cobs, and set aside. Pile grilled peppers, onions, hot peppers, garlic, and lime juice in a food processor and purée until smooth. In a very large bowl, combine this purée with vinegar, tomato juice, clam juice, and reserved vegetables. Add cumin, cilantro, sugar, salt, and pepper. Refrigerate for at least 8 hours. Serve with croutons and avocado.

YIELD: 8 TO 10 SERVINGS

Shrimp Soup

1 pound shrimp
5 tablespoons unsalted butter
2½ tablespoons flour
½ teaspoon mace
1 teaspoon salt
½ teaspoon onion powder
Garlic powder, to taste
1 teaspoon Worcestershire sauce
2½ cups hot milk
2 to 4 tablespoons dry sherry

Drop shrimp into boiling water and remove as soon as water returns to a boil. Peel shrimp, place in the bowl of a food processor, and pulse only until shrimp are chopped into fairly small pieces. Melt butter in the top of a double boiler over hot water and whisk in flour until well combined; let the mixture bubble for a minute. Stir in mace, salt, onion powder, garlic powder, Worcestershire sauce, and hot milk. Add shrimp and cook in the double boiler for 5 to 7 minutes to bring out the flavor of the shrimp, but do not let soup come to a boil. Add sherry just before serving.

YIELD: 4 SERVINGS

This soup can be made a day ahead. To reheat, use a double boiler again; otherwise, the soup may curdle.

Elegant Crab Bisque

1 pound fresh crabmeat
¼ cup butter
1 teaspoon salt
½ teaspoon white pepper
2 cups milk
2 cups light cream
½ teaspoon Tabasco sauce
1 teaspoon Worcestershire sauce
6 tablespoons dry sherry
Lemon slices
Parsley sprigs

Bring crabmeat, butter, salt, pepper, and milk to a slow simmer and cook for 10 minutes. Add cream, Tabasco sauce, and Worcestershire sauce and bring to a simmer but do not boil; simmer about 15 minutes. Stir as little as possible so as not to break up the crabmeat. Remove from the heat, add sherry, and serve in warm soup plates or cups with lemon slices and parsley.

YIELD: 4 SERVINGS

Stews

Simple Seafood Stew

2 dozen medium shrimp,
  shelled and deveined
1 pound cod fillet, cut into
  1½-inch cubes (boneless
  thick end)
4 garlic cloves, minced
¼ cup extra virgin olive oil,
  divided
2 large onions, chopped
2 large yellow bell peppers,
  seeded and cut into strips
  3 inches long and ¼ inch
  wide
2 tablespoons tomato paste
2 cups clam juice
4 cups canned whole tomatoes,
  cut up and liquid reserved
1 lemon, thinly sliced
¼ teaspoon dried thyme leaves
¼ teaspoon dried basil
¼ teaspoon dried oregano
¼ teaspoon dried sage
½ teaspoon red pepper flakes
Salt, to taste
Pepper, to taste
24 mussels, scrubbed and
  debearded
⅔ cup dry vermouth or dry
  white wine
¼ cup minced flatleaf parsley

In a small bowl, toss shrimp and cod with garlic and 1 tablespoon oil, and let stand while preparing the base. In a 3-quart saucepan, cook onions and peppers in remaining 3 tablespoons oil, stirring until beginning to turn golden. Add tomato paste and cook over moderately low heat, stirring, for 3 minutes. Add clam juice in a stream and simmer, stirring, until mixture has thickened slightly. Stir in tomatoes with their liquid, lemon slices, thyme, basil, oregano, sage, red pepper flakes, salt, and pepper. Simmer 10 minutes. While the stew is simmering, combine mussels and vermouth in a 2-quart saucepan and bring to a boil. Steam, covered, 3 to 5 minutes, or until mussels have opened; discard any unopened ones. Add shrimp and cod mixture to stew and simmer 5 minutes or until cod is just cooked through. Add mussels with their cooking liquid and parsley and heat until mussels are warmed.

YIELD: 6 SERVINGS

PIERRE NICHON, active in 1645–1655
After Sebastian Stoskopff, born in Strasbourg,
about 1596–1657
Still Life with a Dead Carp on a Box

A Taste of New England

Treat friends and family to typical New England fare by preparing a seafood stew or chowder, or capture the flavors of New England with a menu drawn from these selections:

- Boston Baked Beans (page 146) and Boston Brown Bread (page 74)
- Succotash with a Dash (page 139)
- Baked Scrod with Crumb Topping (page 93), Cape Cod Bluefish (page 91), or Swordfish Nantucket (page 90)
- New England Boiled Dinner (page 111) and Irish Soda Bread (page 77)
- Yankee Pot Roast (page 110) and Parker House Rolls (page 80)
- Baked Indian Pudding (page 165), Big Dig Mud (page 177), Boston Cream Pie (page 178), or Maple Syrup Pudding Cake (page 165)

Hearty Fisherman's Stew

1 tablespoon extra virgin
    olive oil
1 (6-ounce) chorizo sausage,
    sliced ¼ inch thick
1 medium fennel bulb, halved
    and julienned
2 large onions, chopped
3 bell peppers (1 yellow, 1 red,
    and 1 green), seeded and
    cut in 1½-inch slices
5 garlic cloves, peeled
3½ cups canned tomatoes
    in tomato purée
2 cups clam juice
1½ cups dry white wine
1 teaspoon salt
¼ teaspoon red pepper flakes,
    or to taste
1 pound boneless cod fillets,
    thick end, cut in 1½-inch
    cubes
1 pound medium shrimp,
    shelled and deveined
1 pound littleneck clams
¼ cup chopped parsley

In a 6-quart stockpot, heat olive oil and cook chorizo over medium heat until the sausage has browned and fat is rendered. Remove chorizo from the pot; set aside. Pour off all but a thin film of fat. Add fennel, onions, peppers, and garlic and cook over medium-low heat until onions and peppers are tender, about 10 minutes. Add tomatoes, breaking them up with a spoon, and then clam juice, wine, salt, and red pepper flakes. Heat to boiling over high heat. Reduce heat to low, cover, and simmer 30 minutes. Add chorizo and cod and simmer 4 minutes. Add shrimp and clams and simmer 3 minutes, or until shrimp curl and clams open. Discard any unopened clams. To serve, remove garlic, ladle soup into wide bowls, and garnish with parsley.

YIELD: 6 SERVINGS

Chowders

Oven Fish Chowder

2 pounds haddock or similar
  white fish, cut in 2-inch
  pieces
4 medium potatoes, peeled
  and sliced
A few chopped celery leaves
2 bay leaves
2½ teaspoons kosher salt
4 whole cloves
1 clove garlic, peeled
  and crushed
3 onions, sliced
½ cup butter
2 cups boiling water
½ cup dry white wine
¼ teaspoon dried dill seed
¼ teaspoon white pepper
2 cups light cream

Put all ingredients, except cream, in a large covered baking dish and bake in a preheated 375-degree oven for 1 hour. Discard bay leaves. Heat cream to scalding and add to chowder. Serve immediately or—even better—the next day.

YIELD: 6 SERVINGS

New England Seafood Chowder

3 tablespoons extra virgin
   olive oil

1 onion, chopped

2 cloves garlic, minced

1 red or green bell pepper,
   seeded and chopped

1 leek, rinsed and chopped

2 carrots, scraped and chopped

½ teaspoon red pepper flakes,
   or Tabasco sauce to taste

1 bay leaf

½ teaspoon dried thyme leaves

1 cup vermouth

2 cups canned diced tomatoes

½ pound potatoes, cut in
   ½-inch cubes

1 to 2 cups clam juice

⅔ pound scallops, cut in half
   if large

1½ pounds white fish (sea bass,
   scrod, halibut), cut in
   2-inch pieces

½ pound fresh lobster meat
   (optional)

1 cup light or heavy cream

¼ cup minced parsley

Salt, to taste

Pepper, to taste

Heat oil in a large stockpot and sauté onion, garlic, bell pepper, leek, and carrots until vegetables are tender. Add red pepper flakes, bay leaf, thyme, vermouth, and tomatoes and bring to a boil. Add potatoes, return soup to a boil, and cook for about 15 minutes, or until potatoes are done. Add clam juice and cook, uncovered, for 5 minutes. (Recipe can be prepared to this point a day or so in advance. Bring soup to a simmer before proceeding with the recipe.) Add seafood and cook 2 to 3 minutes only. Do not overcook or the fish will fall apart. Add cream and bring just to a boil. Gently stir in parsley, salt, and pepper.

YIELD: 6 SERVINGS

As an added touch, rub a loaf of French bread with garlic, slice thinly, brush with extra virgin olive oil, and brown under the broiler. Place one of the slices in each bowl and add chowder.

Sweet Potato Chowder

8 sweet potatoes or garnet yams

2 large yellow onions, coarsely
chopped

1 head garlic, separated into
cloves, peeled, and coarsely
chopped

3 tablespoons vegetable oil

1 tablespoon cumin

3 tablespoons chopped cilantro

½ teaspoon ground red pepper

4 cups vegetable stock

3 cups orange juice

Juice of 3 to 4 limes

2 teaspoons salt, or to taste

Pepper, to taste

Additional chopped cilantro

1 medium Bermuda or Spanish
onion, caramelized

Prick potatoes with a fork, place on a foil-lined baking pan, and bake until soft. When potatoes have cooled, remove the skins and mash coarsely. While the potatoes are baking, slowly and gently cook onions and garlic in oil over medium heat for 5 minutes, or until they wilt and become translucent; add cumin, cilantro, and ground red pepper. Cook over low heat until flavors have blended, about 10 minutes. Add potatoes to onion mixture and stir well. Add vegetable stock and simmer, partially covered, for 20 minutes. Add orange and lime juices; cover and simmer for an additional 10 minutes. Season with salt and pepper. Serve in individual soup bowls and garnish with cilantro and caramelized onion.

YIELD: 8 TO 10 SERVINGS

To caramelize an onion, slice it as thinly as possible and slowly brown in a skillet with 3 tablespoons balsamic vinegar and 1 tablespoon brown sugar until onion is crisp at the edges and almost blackened.

Salads, Dressings, Seasonings

When to serve the salad? Will it be at each place as the guests are seated, or will it follow the main course? Is your salad hearty enough to be an entrée itself? Today we enjoy many varieties of greens and edible flowers. You can add interest with seeds, nuts, fruits, seafood—the possibilities are legion. Combine the salad with a favorite fresh dressing, perhaps with Asian flavorings, and present it in a fabulous bowl.

Bench, 1998
Made by ERIC O'LEARY, born 1949

Salads

Mesclun Greens with Pine Nuts

½ cup pine nuts
Mesclun greens to serve 4
¼ cup extra virgin olive oil,
    or just enough to coat greens
Juice of ½ lemon
Kosher or sea salt, to taste

Toast pine nuts in an oven or skillet until light brown; watch carefully. Put greens in a bowl and toss with olive oil and lemon juice. Add salt and pine nuts and mix well.

YIELD: 4 SERVINGS

Because of their high oil content, pine nuts are quick to burn when left unattended.

Mesclun Greens with Goat Cheese and Candied Walnuts

1 (8-ounce) log peppered goat
    cheese, cut into 8 slices
Extra virgin olive oil
Mesclun greens to serve 8

CANDIED WALNUTS
1½ cups walnut halves
1½ teaspoons water
2 tablespoons light brown sugar
⅛ teaspoon kosher salt

SHERRY VINAIGRETTE
1 medium shallot, minced
½ to 1 teaspoon Dijon mustard
2 tablespoons sherry wine
    vinegar
⅛ teaspoon kosher salt
⅛ teaspoon cracked pepper
½ to 1 teaspoon chopped thyme
½ cup extra virgin olive oil

Toast walnuts in a preheated 350-degree oven until light brown; transfer to a bowl. Add water, sugar, and salt and toss. Spread nuts on a baking sheet lined with parchment paper and bake at 350 degrees until brown; let cool.

To make vinaigrette, combine shallot, mustard, vinegar, salt, pepper, and thyme; gradually whisk in oil.

Preheat broiler. Set the goat cheese slices on a baking sheet, brush with olive oil, and broil for 1 minute or until warmed through. Toss greens with vinaigrette, add walnuts, mound salad on individual plates, and top each serving with a slice of warm goat cheese.

YIELD: 8 SERVINGS

Double the recipe for candied walnuts and freeze the extra batch for use with other dishes.

Field Greens, Roasted Tomatoes, and Jicama

1 pint grape tomatoes

1 tablespoon extra virgin
 olive oil

1 teaspoon coarse salt

1 teaspoon freshly ground
 black pepper

1 medium jicama, peeled and
 finely julienned

Field greens to serve 6

VINAIGRETTE

2 tablespoons red wine vinegar

1 teaspoon Dijon mustard

1 tablespoon honey

½ teaspoon salt

½ teaspoon freshly ground
 black pepper

⅓ cup extra virgin olive oil

Rinse tomatoes and remove stems. Roast tomatoes in a preheated 400-degree oven for 3 minutes. Gently fold tomatoes into oil, salt, and pepper; refrigerate tomato mixture and jicama until needed. In a blender or food processor, combine vinegar, mustard, honey, salt, and pepper at medium speed; slowly add olive oil. Spread greens on a platter and top with tomato mixture, jicama, and vinaigrette.

YIELD: 6 SERVINGS

UNIDENTIFIED ARTIST, mid-19th century
Tomatoes, Fruit, and Flowers, about 1860

Edible Flowers

Enjoy edible flowers with your favorite appetizers, salads, and desserts. There is nothing so lovely as a spray of fresh flowers decorating a cake or individual blossoms garnishing a salad or beverage. You can avoid health risks by insisting on organically grown flowers, rinsing them thoroughly, and selecting only from this list:

Carnation	Gardenia	Pansy
Chrysanthemum	Honeysuckle	Peony
Cornflower	Lavender	Rose
Daisy	Marigold	Viola
Daylily	Nasturtium	Violet

To sugar the petals for use in a dessert, first dip them into frothy egg whites and then into superfine sugar and set on a rack to dry. If you don't have superfine sugar on hand, pulse ordinary granulated sugar in a food processor to make it finer. Nasturtium blossoms can be filled with flavored cream cheese and served as hors d'oeuvres.

Panzanella

4 cups bite-size pieces crusty
    bread
3 large, ripe tomatoes, seeded
    and cut into ¾-inch pieces
    (about 3 cups)
¼ cup finely chopped Bermuda
    or Spanish onion
⅓ cup pitted and chopped
    Kalamata olives
2 tablespoons drained capers
2 to 3 tablespoons red wine
    or balsamic vinegar
2 cloves garlic, mashed to
    a paste in a mortar with
    ½ teaspoon salt
1 tablespoon Dijon mustard
⅓ cup extra virgin olive oil
Salt, to taste
Pepper, to taste
1 cup basil leaves, torn
    into pieces

Arrange bread in one layer on a jellyroll pan and toast about 5 inches below a preheated broiler with the door open, until golden brown, about 1 minute on each side. Watch carefully. Remove bread from the pan and let cool. Toss bread with tomatoes, onion, olives, and capers. In a blender or food processor, blend vinegar, garlic paste, mustard, oil, salt, and pepper until smooth. Just before serving, drizzle vinaigrette over salad, mix in basil, and toss well.

YIELD: 6 SERVINGS

Bowl
China, Qing dynasty, Kangxi period,
early 18th century

Green Beans with Sesame Dressing

DRESSING
¼ cup white sesame seeds,
    toasted and ground
    into paste
1 tablespoon sake
1 tablespoon sugar
1 tablespoon soy sauce

1 pound green beans, ends
    and strings removed
⅛ teaspoon salt

Toast sesame seeds in a skillet or toaster oven, stirring occasionally, until they begin to pop. (Do not let seeds burn; they will make the dressing bitter.) Grind seeds in a blender or with a mortar and pestle to make a paste. Add sake, sugar, and soy sauce and mix well. Thinly slice beans on the diagonal into 2-inch lengths. Cook in boiling salted water until beans are crisp-tender and bright green, about 3 to 5 minutes. Toss beans in the dressing and serve warm or at room temperature.

YIELD: 4 SERVINGS

This dressing also goes well with most cooked vegetables.

Black Bean Salad

2 (15-ounce) cans black beans,
    rinsed and drained
½ cup chopped celery
1 English cucumber, chopped
3 carrots, chopped
4 plum tomatoes, seeded and
    chopped
1 bunch scallions, chopped
1 (4½-ounce) can green chiles,
    chopped
½ cup chopped cilantro
1 tablespoon cumin seeds,
    roasted

3 tablespoons white wine vinegar
Juice of 4 limes
1 cup fresh corn kernels, uncooked
1 cup chopped red bell pepper
3 tablespoons extra virgin olive oil
Salt, to taste
Pepper, to taste

Place all ingredients in a large bowl and mix.

YIELD: 8 SERVINGS

To roast cumin seeds, put them in a skillet over high heat and shake pan gently until seeds turn brown.

Bed quilt
American, 1830s

Beet Salad with Walnuts and Baked Goat Cheese

¼ cup extra virgin olive oil

2 tablespoons balsamic vinegar

2 tablespoons water

I clove garlic, minced

I tablespoon chopped mint
   or dill

I teaspoon salt

I teaspoon freshly ground
   black pepper

I pound beets, peeled and
   cut into large wedges

I medium Spanish onion,
   peeled, halved, and thickly
   sliced

¼ cup extra virgin olive oil

½ cup dried bread crumbs

I teaspoon dried thyme leaves

I (8-ounce) log goat cheese,
   cut into 8 slices

½ cup walnut halves, toasted

Combine oil, vinegar, water, garlic, mint, salt, and pepper in a small bowl. Place beets and onion in a large baking pan; toss with oil mixture. Cover and bake in a preheated 350-degree oven for I hour, or until beets are tender. Chill well. Put oil in a flat dish; mix bread crumbs and thyme in another. Coat each side of cheese rounds first in oil and then in crumbs. Place rounds on an oiled baking sheet and bake in a preheated 400-degree oven for 6 minutes, or until cheese is lightly bubbling and golden. (If you over-bake the rounds, they will lose their shape.) Drain beet mixture, divide into servings, and garnish with cheese and walnuts.

YIELD: 8 SERVINGS

Greek Peasant Salad

2 to 3 cups cherry tomatoes,
   halved

2 cups chopped, seeded
   cucumber

½ medium red onion, thinly
   sliced

½ cup crumbled feta

½ teaspoon salt

Freshly ground pepper, to taste

Extra virgin olive oil

Put tomatoes, cucumber, onion, and cheese in large bowl. Sprinkle with salt and pepper; drizzle with olive oil. Toss lightly to combine and serve immediately.

YIELD: 4 SERVINGS

This salad lends itself to the addition of fresh herbs like oregano or basil.

Summer Salad

1 pint grape tomatoes, halved
4 celery ribs, chopped
½ red onion, sliced
2 bunches arugula, torn into
  bite-size pieces
2¾ cups fresh corn kernels,
  uncooked
⅓ cup extra virgin olive oil
2 tablespoons balsamic vinegar
Salt, to taste
Pepper, to taste
1 cup crumbled blue cheese,
  divided

Combine tomatoes, celery, onion, arugula, and corn in glass bowl. Whisk together oil and vinegar. Add salt, pepper, and ¾ cup of cheese. Mix well and toss with salad. Garnish with remaining cheese.

YIELD: 8 TO 10 SERVINGS

Cranberry Carrot Salad

3 cups shredded carrots
  (about 1 pound)
1½ cups celery, thinly sliced
  on the diagonal
1 cup coarsely chopped
  cranberries
½ cup chopped walnuts
⅓ cup vegetable oil
3 tablespoons orange juice
3 tablespoons cider vinegar
2 tablespoons honey
½ teaspoon salt
⅛ teaspoon pepper

In a medium bowl, combine carrots, celery, cranberries, and walnuts. In a small bowl, whisk together oil, orange juice, vinegar, honey, salt, and pepper until well blended. Pour over salad; toss well. Cover salad and chill at least 2 hours.

YIELD: 8 SERVINGS

JOHN SINGLETON COPLEY, 1738–1815
Mrs. Ezekiel Goldthwait (Elizabeth Lewis), 1771

Citrus Salad

4 medium blood or navel
    oranges
2 medium very ripe lemons
    (optional)
1 small red onion, peeled
    and thinly sliced
8 mint or basil leaves, finely
    chopped
Freshly ground black pepper,
    to taste
2 tablespoons extra virgin
    olive oil
Mint sprigs or basil leaves
    for garnish

Peel oranges and lemons, if using, removing the white pith completely. (Peel over a plate to catch and reserve the juices.) Slice oranges about ¼ inch thick; slice lemons about ⅛ inch thick. Spread oranges on a platter and arrange lemons over them in a neat pattern. Pour on juice collected from the peeling and slicing. Top with onion and sprinkle with mint and pepper. Drizzle the entire surface with oil and let the platter stand for about 2 hours at room temperature before serving. Garnish with mint sprigs.

YIELD: 4 TO 6 SERVINGS

For an interesting texture, add thinly sliced cucumber or radish before topping with onion.

Solar Summer Salad

⅔ cup extra virgin olive oil
2 cups torn basil leaves, divided
2 to 3 cups cherry tomatoes,
    halved
½ cup capers
1½ cups pitted Kalamata olives
⅛ teaspoon garlic powder,
    or to taste
1 pound medium shell pasta
1 to 1½ cups feta
Salt, to taste
Pepper, to taste
Red pepper flakes, to taste
¼ to ½ cup finely sliced red
    onion (optional)
Freshly grated Parmesan,
    to taste

In large bowl, mix olive oil, 1 cup basil leaves, tomatoes, capers, olives, and garlic powder; place directly in the sun for 5 to 6 hours. (If no sun is available, you can place the mixture in a 200- to 225-degree oven instead, but the flavor will not be the same. The idea is to not break down the tomatoes.) Just before serving, cook shells al dente. Toss drained pasta with solar mixture; add feta, remaining 1 cup basil, seasonings, onion, and Parmesan. Serve hot or at room temperature.

YIELD: 6 SERVINGS

Chicken and Two Rice Salad

4 cups chicken stock

1 cup wild rice, rinsed

1 cup long grain brown rice

2 whole boneless, skinless
    chicken breasts, cooked
    and cubed

½ cup coarsely chopped
    pecans, toasted

3 scallions, sliced

½ cup golden raisins

½ cup chopped celery

2 teaspoons grated orange peel

2 tablespoons minced chives

ORANGE VINAIGRETTE

¼ cup white wine vinegar

¼ cup orange juice

2 tablespoons Dijon mustard

2 tablespoons mango chutney,
    chopped

½ teaspoon salt

¼ teaspoon white pepper

½ cup extra virgin olive oil

In a large saucepan, bring chicken stock to a boil. Stir in wild rice and simmer, covered, for 10 minutes. Add brown rice and continue to simmer mixture for approximately 45 minutes, or until liquid is absorbed. Remove from heat and cool to room temperature. In a large bowl, combine rice, chicken, pecans, scallions, raisins, celery, and peel.

Mix vinegar, juice, mustard, chutney, salt, and pepper in small bowl. Add oil in a slow, steady stream, whisking constantly until slightly thickened and thoroughly combined. Add to rice mixture, tossing gently to combine. Sprinkle with chives and serve at room temperature.

YIELD: 6 SERVINGS

This recipe is a good way to use leftover chicken. It may be made the night before and refrigerated.

Lobster Salad

2 red bell peppers

I pound red potatoes, cooked
and cut into ⅓-inch-thick
slices

2 cups fresh corn kernels,
uncooked

Boston Bibb lettuce

I pound cooked, chilled lobster
meat, cut into ½-inch-thick
slices

2 tablespoons chopped dill

DRESSING

¼ cup rice vinegar

¼ cup extra virgin olive oil

6 to 8 scallions, thinly sliced

Salt, to taste

Freshly ground pepper, to taste

Place peppers in a roasting pan and char them under the broiler until blackened on all sides; turn occasionally until they collapse, about 10 to 20 minutes. Place peppers in a paper bag and let stand 10 minutes to steam. Let peppers cool; then peel, seed, and dice. To make the dressing, in a small bowl whisk together vinegar and oil. Mix in scallions, salt, and pepper and set aside. Put potatoes, corn, and peppers in a large bowl, and toss with half the dressing. Arrange beds of lettuce on four chilled serving plates. Divide potato mixture onto lettuce, and top each serving with lobster. Just before serving, drizzle with remaining dressing and garnish with fresh dill.

YIELD: 4 SERVINGS

Most New Englanders prefer their lobster simply prepared, either boiled or broiled, with a squeeze of fresh lemon and some melted butter for dipping. A typical lobster salad consists of lobster meat, with just enough mayonnaise to moisten, served on a bed of lettuce or in a toasted hot dog bun. This recipe is a delightful departure from the usual plain Yankee taste.

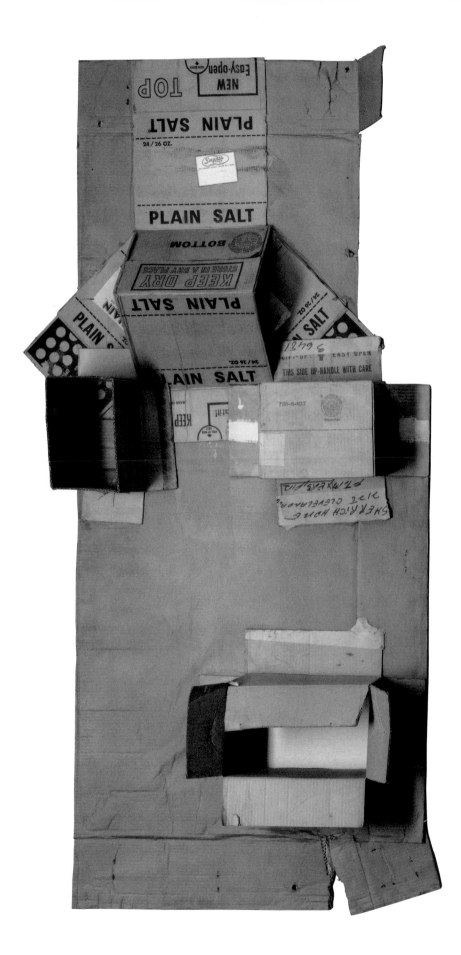

Dressings

One-Minute Blender Mayonnaise

1 egg
1 teaspoon lemon juice
½ teaspoon salt
½ teaspoon dry mustard
1 cup vegetable oil or mixed
　with extra virgin olive oil

Place egg, lemon juice, salt, and mustard in a blender; cover and run at medium speed for 10 seconds. While the blender is still running, remove the cover and add a small amount of oil. After a few seconds, pour a thin stream of oil into the blender, making sure oil emulsifies as you pour. This process will take less than a minute, and the mayonnaise may thicken enough before you have used all the oil.

YIELD: 1 ¼ CUPS

To create a special flavor, mix in some Herb Salt (page 70) or French Spice Mix (page 71). For a different variation, add ⅓ cup chopped dill after adding all the oil. To make green mayonnaise, add 10 sprigs water-cress, 10 leaves spinach, or 10 stalks tarragon.

Curry Chutney Mayonnaise

1 tablespoon safflower oil
½ onion, finely chopped
2 tablespoons curry powder
1 cup One-Minute Blender
　Mayonnaise (above)
Juice of 1 lime
2 tablespoons sour cream
2 tablespoons mango chutney,
　chopped

Heat oil in a small skillet and sauté onion over low heat until soft, 8 to 10 minutes. Add curry powder and cook, stirring, for 5 minutes. Cool completely. Add lime juice, sour cream, and chutney. Stir well. Blend mayonnaise into mixture. Refrigerate until ready to serve.

YIELD: 1 ½ CUPS

ROBERT RAUSCHENBERG,
Plain Salt (Cardboards), 1971

Wasabi Mayonnaise

1 large egg yolk, room
    temperature
⅓ teaspoon salt
2 teaspoons rice vinegar
1 tablespoon wasabi powder
½ cup vegetable oil
1 tablespoon lime juice

In a small bowl, whisk together egg yolk, salt, rice vinegar, and wasabi powder until well blended. Slowly add vegetable oil, beating vigorously, until mixture thickens. Whisk in lime juice. Cover mayonnaise with plastic wrap and let it rest for 10 minutes before using.

YIELD: ½ TO ⅔ CUP

This mayonnaise goes well with many foods—potatoes, vegetables, seafood, poultry, meats. Try it with Salmon Crab Cakes (page 31) or Marinated Mussels (page 30).

Cucumber Horseradish Dressing

1 cucumber, peeled, seeded,
    and finely diced (about
    ¾ cup)
¾ cup sour cream
3 tablespoons drained bottled
    horseradish
1 teaspoon white wine vinegar
2 teaspoons minced rosemary
    leaves

Whisk together all ingredients, season with salt and pepper, and chill for 2 to 24 hours.

YIELD: 1¾ CUPS

Crème Fraîche

1 cup heavy cream
1 cup sour cream

Whisk heavy and sour creams together in a bowl. Cover loosely with plastic wrap and let stand overnight or until thickened. In cold weather, this can take as long as 24 hours. Cover well and refrigerate for at least 4 hours, after which the crème fraîche will be quite thick.

YIELD: 2 CUPS

Covered bowl and stand
France (Vincennes Factory), 1754

Seasonings

Herb Salt

1 cup salt
2½ teaspoons paprika
2 teaspoons dry mustard
1 teaspoon curry powder
½ (or more) teaspoon each:
  onion powder
  garlic powder
  dried oregano
  dried parsley
  dried thyme leaves
  dried rosemary

Sieve or grind in mortar with pestle to crush herbs. Amounts may be varied to taste and purpose, using other herbs.

YIELD: 1½ CUPS

Excellent on eggs or salads, this versatile mix enhances almost any dish.

Curry Powder

4 teaspoons dried coriander
2 teaspoons turmeric
1 teaspoon cumin
1 teaspoon dry mustard
1 teaspoon ground ginger
1 teaspoon chili powder
1 teaspoon cinnamon
1 teaspoon ground cardamom
½ teaspoon white pepper

Blend all ingredients and store in airtight container.

YIELD: 4 TABLESPOONS

Use with Cold Senegalese Soup (page 40) and West Indian Curry (page 123). Many cooks add a pinch of curry powder to enhance everyday dishes like chicken soup, stuffed eggs, or shrimp salad.

French Spice Mix

2 cups white pepper

⅓ cup cayenne

⅓ cup mace

2 tablespoons cinnamon

2 tablespoons cloves

2 tablespoons ground
   marjoram

2 tablespoons nutmeg

2 tablespoons dried basil

2 tablespoons dried rosemary

2 tablespoons dried thyme
   leaves

Mix spices and herbs thoroughly. Store in airtight jar. Use as a "meat rub" or poultry seasoning, with soups and vegetables, or add a pinch to baked products. Note: For the basil, rosemary, or thyme in this recipe, you can substitute 2 tablespoons dried sage, coriander, or tarragon.

YIELD: 3½ CUPS

To add a personal touch to your food preparation, create your own spice and herb mixture. Use a small amount (¼ teaspoon) of the blend, with a touch of pepper for bite or heat, to impart a unique depth and aroma to your dishes.

Brunch or Lunch

Transform lunch or brunch into a special occasion with an inventive soup and salad combination or with one of the following accompanied by mixed field greens and bread or rolls:

· Linguine with Seared Shrimp (page 127)
· Chicken and Two Rice Salad (page 64) or Lobster Salad (page 65)
· Caramelized Onion Quesadillas (page 30) or Smoked Salmon and
   Dill Quesadilla (page 131)
· Asian Stuffed Portobello Mushrooms (page 99)
· Salmon Crab Cakes (page 31)
· Savory Cheese Tart (page 130)
· Soufflé Sandwich with Crabmeat (page 130)

Breads,
Rolls,
Sandwiches

How many times do we vow not to eat any bread, only to have our resolve vanish as we are once again seduced by the staff of life? You may choose to serve a whole delicious loaf, waiting to be sliced on an attractive bread board, or a basket filled with assorted fresh warm breads and rolls. Sandwiches that start with homemade bread please guests of all ages.

Settee, 1979
Made by WENDELL CASTLE, born 1932

Breads

Boston Brown Bread

1 cup flour
2 cups yellow cornmeal
1 teaspoon salt
2½ teaspoons baking soda
¾ cup molasses
2 cups buttermilk
½ cup raisins (optional)

Sift together flour, cornmeal, salt, and baking soda into a large mixing bowl. In another bowl, whisk together molasses and buttermilk; add to the dry ingredients. Add raisins to the batter, if desired. Stir until batter is well blended and pour into a well greased lidded mold (1 to 1½ quarts), filling not more than two-thirds full. Grease the inside of the lid before putting it on. (A mold without a lid may be covered with greased heavy aluminum foil, greased side down, and secured with string.) Set the mold on a rack in a deep stockpot; pour in boiling water to come halfway up the mold. Cover the kettle, bring water to a boil, and then turn down the heat so that the water simmers gently. Steam bread for 3½ hours. Add more water as needed to keep the correct water level. Remove mold from the water onto a rack, uncover the bread, and allow it to cool 15 to 20 minutes before unmolding. To use a pressure cooker, set the mold on the rack in the cooker. Add 2 inches of water. Steam for 15 minutes with the petcock open; close it and steam for 1 hour.

YIELD: 10 TO 12 SERVINGS

Traditionally served warm with Boston Baked Beans (page 146), brown bread can be reheated in a 300-degree oven. It is also delicious toasted for breakfast.

Sun-dried Tomato Herb Bread

3½ cups flour

2 tablespoons sugar

2 teaspoons salt

2 teaspoons baking soda

1 teaspoon basil

¼ teaspoon French Spice Mix
   (page 71)

¼ teaspoon dried thyme leaves

¼ cup butter, softened

1¾ cups buttermilk

½ cup drained sun-dried
   tomatoes packed in oil,
   patted dry and cut into
   pieces

Mix flour, sugar, salt, baking soda, basil, French spice mix, and thyme in a bowl. Using a fork, blend butter into flour mixture; add buttermilk and sun-dried tomatoes. Stir until all flour is dampened. Batter will be stiff but sticky. Flour your hands and shape dough into a round 8 to 9 inches in diameter. Place into a well greased, 2-quart round baking dish; and with a sharp knife, cut an X, about ½ inch deep, into the top of the loaf. Bake in a preheated 400-degree oven for 30 to 35 minutes, or until nicely brown and a tester inserted in the center comes out clean. Remove from the pan and cool on a rack before slicing.

YIELD: 1 LOAF

Walnut Onion Bread

3 cups flour

⅓ cup sugar

1 tablespoon baking powder

½ teaspoon baking soda

1 teaspoon salt

1 cup chopped walnuts, divided

1½ cups buttermilk

¼ cup butter, melted

½ cup minced onion

Combine flour, sugar, baking powder, baking soda, and salt. Stir in ¾ cup walnuts. Mix in buttermilk, butter, and onion until dough is evenly moist. Turn dough into a greased, 9-inch round baking dish, sprinkle top with remaining walnuts, and bake in a preheated 350-degree oven for 40 to 45 minutes, or until brown and a tester inserted in the center comes out clean. Let stand in the pan for 5 minutes; turn out onto a rack to cool.

YIELD: 1 LOAF

Irish Soda Bread

3½ cups flour

2 tablespoons sugar

2 teaspoons salt

2 teaspoons baking soda

¼ cup butter, softened

1¾ cups buttermilk

1 cup raisins

2 tablespoons caraway seeds
  (optional)

Mix flour, sugar, salt, and baking soda in a bowl. Using a fork, blend butter into flour mixture; add buttermilk, raisins, and caraway seeds, if desired. Stir until all flour is dampened. Batter will be stiff but sticky. Flour your hands and shape dough into a round 8 to 9 inches in diameter. Place into a well greased, 2-quart round baking dish; and with a sharp knife, cut an X, about ½ inch deep, into the top of the loaf. Bake in a preheated 400-degree oven for 30 to 35 minutes, or until nicely brown and a tester inserted in the center comes out clean. Remove from the pan and cool on a rack before slicing.

YIELD: 1 LOAF

This rich, tender quick bread makes an ideal companion for New England Boiled Dinner (page 111). To make brown soda bread, substitute 2¾ cups whole wheat flour for an equal amount of the white flour and eliminate the raisins.

Yeast Bread Hints

The amount of flour required will vary each time you bake, because humidity affects the composition of flour at various times of the year. Near the end of the mixing process, add the remaining flour 1 cup at a time, until the dough forms a mass and cleans the side of the bowl. The dough should be easy to handle but somewhat sticky. Turn it onto a lightly floured surface to be kneaded.

Kneading for 8 to 10 minutes allows the flour and liquid to develop the gluten that creates a smooth and elastic bread dough. To knead by hand, flour your hands and use a rhythmic push-fold-turn motion. With the heels of your hands, push the dough against the floured surface away from you; then fold the dough to the center toward you, and rotate it a quarter turn. Continue in this manner, sprinkling additional flour on the surface if the dough sticks to your hands or work surface. Break the rhythm occasionally by slamming the dough against the work surface.

Form the dough into a ball and place it in a large, clean greased bowl; turn it to coat the entire surface and prevent a dry crust from forming. Cover the bowl with plastic wrap or a hot damp towel. Set it in a warm (80 to 85 degrees) draft-free location until doubled in bulk. To determine when the dough has doubled in bulk, lightly press two fingertips into it; if the impressions remain, it has doubled. The dough should double in bulk in about 1¼ to 2 hours. Do not use this test on dough that has been shaped into loaves or rolls.

Punch down the dough by pushing your fist into the center, pulling the edges to the center, and turning the dough over to form a ball. Some recipes call for another rising to create a finer grain. It should double again in about 30 to 60 minutes.

After the first or second rising—whichever is called for—knead the ball of dough for 2 to 3 minutes to eliminate air pockets. Add more flour if necessary for easier handling. Gently divide the dough and shape it into loaves or rolls. Cover the shaped dough lightly with a towel and allow it to double again, about 45 minutes.

Bake on the center rack of the oven, using the temperature and time suggested in the recipe. The bread should be evenly browned. (As a test for doneness, the bottom sounds hollow when tapped.) Remove the bread from the pans promptly and cool on wire racks.

To enhance the look and flavor of the crust, you can brush it with melted butter immediately after removing it from the oven, or make an egg wash by whisking 1 egg with 2 teaspoons of water and brush it over the bread before baking.

Shredded Wheat Bread

½ teaspoon sugar

2 packages active dry yeast
   (4½ teaspoons)

½ cup warm water (105 to
   115 degrees)

2 shredded wheat biscuits

2 cups boiling water

1 tablespoon salt

2 tablespoons sugar

3 tablespoons butter

5 to 5½ cups unbleached flour

2 tablespoons butter, room
   temperature

Dissolve sugar and yeast in warm water. Break shredded wheat into a large bowl and add boiling water, salt, sugar, and butter. When mixture has cooled slightly, add dissolved yeast and stir in flour. Turn dough out onto a floured surface and knead 8 to 10 minutes, until it is smooth and elastic. Place dough in a greased bowl, turning to coat the entire surface. Cover the bowl with a warm damp cloth and let the dough rise in a warm, draft-free place until doubled in bulk, about 2 hours. Punch down and knead again. Divide the dough in half and place in two greased 9 × 5-inch loaf pans. Let it rise again for 1 hour, until the dough reaches the rims of the pans. Bake in a preheated 350-degree oven for 35 minutes. Turn immediately onto a wire rack, butter the tops of the loaves, and let cool.

YIELD: 2 LOAVES

Dill Bread

1 package active dry yeast
(2¼ teaspoons)
¼ cup warm water (105 to
115 degrees)
1 cup small curd, creamed
cottage cheese, heated to
lukewarm
2 tablespoons sugar
3 tablespoons minced onion
1 tablespoon butter
1 tablespoon chopped dill
or 2 teaspoons dried dill
1 teaspoon salt
¼ teaspoon baking soda
1 egg
2¼ to 2½ cups flour

Soften yeast in water. Combine in a mixing bowl with all other ingredients except flour. Add flour gradually, stirring after each addition, until dough can be handled without sticking. Turn dough out onto a floured surface and knead 8 to 10 minutes, until it is smooth and elastic. Place dough in a greased bowl, turning it to coat the entire surface. Cover the bowl with a warm damp cloth and let rise in a warm, draft-free place until doubled in bulk, about 2 hours. Punch down, remove from the bowl, and place in a well greased 9 × 5-inch loaf pan. Let rise again, about 45 minutes, until the dough is just above the rim of the pan. Bake in a preheated 350-degree oven for 35 to 45 minutes, or until brown. Remove from the pan and let cool on rack.

YIELD: 1 LOAF

Pueblo Bread Bakers, 1984
Made by JOYCE SISNEROS, born 1944

Rolls

Parker House Rolls

½ cup warm water (105 to
115 degrees)

1 package active dry yeast
(2¼ teaspoons)

⅓ cup butter

½ cup boiling water

¼ cup sugar

1 teaspoon salt

1 egg, beaten with a fork

3 cups flour

Butter, melted

Measure water in a small bowl. Add yeast and stir until it has dissolved; set aside. Place butter in a large bowl, add boiling water, and mix until butter is melted. Add sugar, salt, and egg to butter mixture; blend well. Stir in yeast mixture. Add flour and beat until smooth. The dough will be sticky. (If additional flour is needed, add a small amount while kneading.) Turn dough out onto a floured surface and knead 8 to 10 minutes, until it is smooth and elastic. Place dough in a greased bowl, turning to coat the entire surface. Cover the bowl with a warm damp cloth and let dough rise in a warm, draft-free place until doubled in bulk, about 1½ hours. Punch down to form a ball, turn out onto a floured surface, and knead for 2 minutes.

ROLLS: Roll dough out on a floured surface until ¼ inch thick. Cut with a floured 2½-inch round or a special oval cutter and let rounds relax for about 10 minutes. Crease the center of each with the handle of a floured knife or a wooden spoon, brush with melted butter, fold in half, and gently press edges together to seal. For individual rolls, place separately on a lightly greased baking sheet; for pan style, place rolls snugly in greased rimmed pans. Cover rolls with a towel and let rise again for 20 to 30 minutes, or until slightly risen. Bake in a preheated 375-degree oven 12 to 15 minutes for individual rolls, or 20 to 25 minutes for pan style. Brush rolls with melted butter while hot.

YIELD: 2 DOZEN ROLLS

This style of roll, created in the mid-1850s by the bread baker at the famous Parker House Hotel in Boston, has become a traditional American dinner bread.

HORNS: Divide dough in half and roll each half on a floured surface about ¼ inch thick into 12-inch circles. Spread dough with melted butter; sprinkle with cinnamon sugar, if desired. Cut into 12 or 16 pie-shaped pieces depending on desired size. Roll each slice from the wide end to the center. Place on a greased baking sheet with the points down so that horns do not unravel during baking. Cover with a towel and let rise again for 15 to 20 minutes, or until slightly expanded. Bake in a preheated 375-degree oven for 12 to 15 minutes, or until golden. Brush horns with melted butter while hot.

YIELD: 24 TO 32 HORNS

FILLING
3 tablespoons sugar
3 tablespoons brown sugar
1½ teaspoons cinnamon
½ cup raisins
1 cup pecans or walnuts,
    chopped

In a small bowl combine sugars and cinnamon; add raisins and pecans.

TEA RING: Roll dough on a floured surface into an 18 × 9-inch oblong and brush with melted butter; cover dough with filling mixture. Roll up tightly like a jellyroll, beginning at the wide end, and seal by pinching the edges together. Place the roll on a large greased baking sheet with the sealed edge underneath, and pinch the two ends together to form a ring. Using kitchen shears at right angles to the roll, cut dough in slices that are 1 to 1½ inches apart and two-thirds of the way through the ring. As you cut, turn each slice on its side to form a pinwheel design on the baking sheet. Cover the tea ring with a towel and let rise again until doubled in bulk, about 35 to 40 minutes. Bake in a preheated 375-degree oven for 25 to 30 minutes. Brush with melted butter while hot. (Glaze the tea ring with a plain icing while warm and decorate with additional chopped nuts.) Best served warm.

YIELD: 1 TEA RING

Blueberry Buckle

¾ cup sugar

¼ cup unsalted butter

I egg

½ cup milk

2 cups flour

2 teaspoons baking powder

½ teaspoon salt

2 cups fresh blueberries

TOPPING

½ cup sugar

⅓ cup flour

½ to I teaspoon cinnamon

¼ cup cold butter, cut in
    pieces

Blend sugar, butter, and egg in a food processor. Add milk and blend. Sift together flour, baking powder, and salt; combine with butter mixture. Gently stir in blueberries. Spread batter in a greased and floured 9-inch square pan. For the topping, mix sugar, flour, cinnamon, and butter in a food processor just until crumbly; spread evenly over batter. Bake in a preheated 375-degree oven for 45 to 50 minutes.

YIELD: 6 TO 8 SERVINGS

The name Blueberry Buckle dates to Colonial days, when women created recipes calling for blueberries, which are indigenous to North America but were unknown in England. Because a coffee cake with blueberries and streusel topping crumbles easily, cut it into squares and serve it from the pan.

Pumpkin Pancakes

I¾ cups flour

2 tablespoons light brown sugar

2 tablespoons baking powder

I teaspoon salt

2 teaspoons cinnamon

I teaspoon allspice

I½ cups evaporated milk

I cup canned pumpkin

2 eggs, lightly beaten

I½ teaspoons vanilla

¼ cup vegetable oil

Maple syrup, warmed

In a large bowl, combine flour, brown sugar, baking powder, salt, cinnamon, and allspice. Stir in milk, pumpkin, eggs, vanilla, and oil until well blended. Pour the batter onto a lightly oiled, well heated griddle in ⅓-cup measures. Cook about 2 minutes on each side, until golden. Remove to a heated platter. Pass the maple syrup.

YIELD: 18 TO 20 PANCAKES

For variety, dust pancakes with confectioners' sugar and serve with sautéed apple slices.

HENRI MATISSE, 1869–1954
The Three Gourds, about 1916

Popovers

2 eggs, lightly beaten
1 cup milk
1 cup flour
½ teaspoon salt

Beat together all ingredients with a rotary beater until just smooth; do not overbeat. Pour into well greased, deep muffin cups until two-thirds full. (Fill any empty cups one-third to one-half full with water.) Bake in a preheated 425-degree oven until golden brown and crisp on the outside, about 40 to 45 minutes. Give a quick stab to the side of each popover to release the steam, and serve immediately.

YIELD: 5 TO 9 POPOVERS, DEPENDING ON SIZE OF CUP

To use the same recipe for Yorkshire pudding, remove the roast from the oven and drain fat from the pan, reserving ¼ cup. Pour reserved fat into a heated 9-inch square baking pan and add batter. Bake in a preheated 425-degree oven for 35 to 45 minutes, or until golden brown. Do not open oven to check for doneness until the last 5 minutes.

Savory Madeleines

½ cup cornmeal
6 tablespoons flour
1 tablespoon sugar
2 teaspoons baking powder
½ teaspoon salt
Cayenne, to taste
2 tablespoons butter, softened
1 egg
½ cup buttermilk
½ cup Cheddar, shredded
2 tablespoons chopped chives
Crème Fraîche (page 68)
1 (2-ounce) jar red lumpfish
   caviar (about ¼ cup)
Fresh chives

Grease a pan of 2-inch madeleine molds and set aside. In a medium bowl, mix cornmeal, flour, sugar, baking powder, salt, and cayenne until well blended. Add butter, egg, and buttermilk and stir into a batter. Fold in cheese and chives. Spoon enough mixture into each mold so that it just reaches the top. Bake in a preheated 400-degree oven for 6 to 8 minutes, or until brown at edges and slightly rounded on top. Arrange warm madeleines on a serving plate and garnish each with crème fraîche, red lumpfish caviar, and snipped chives. Serve warm or at room temperature.

YIELD: 12 TO 18 MADELEINES

These can be a nice accompaniment to salads and soups or can be served as hors d'oeuvres.

Herbed Dumplings

1 cup flour
2 teaspoons baking powder
½ teaspoon salt
½ cup milk
2 tablespoons vegetable oil
2 tablespoons finely chopped
   parsley or chives

Sift together flour, baking powder, and salt into a mixing bowl. Combine milk, oil, and parsley; add to the dry ingredients, stirring the mixture enough to moisten dough evenly. Gently lay the batter by spoonfuls about ½ inch apart, on top of simmering soup, stew, or salted water. Cover the pan tightly; cook undisturbed for 10 to 15 minutes, until dumplings are firm and dry in the center. If they have been cooked on top of a soup or stew, they are part of that dish. If they have been cooked separately in water, drain with a slotted spoon and serve immediately with melted butter. Dumplings can also be cooked in a well greased steamer, covered, for about 12 minutes.

RUBENS PEALE, 1784–1865
Basket of Fruit, 1860

YIELD: 12 DUMPLINGS

Instead of parsley or chives, you can use the seasoning suggested in a soup or stew recipe.

JEROME B. THOMPSON, 1814–1886
A "Pic Nick," Camden, Maine, about 1850

Sandwiches and More

In addition to the sandwiches in this book, the fancy tea sandwiches in *Boston Tea Parties: Recipes from the Museum of Fine Arts, Boston* can be adapted for any occasion. Choose from canapés, pinwheels, ribbon, lavash, and closed sandwiches to add variety to your list of favorite hors d'oeuvres or to freshen up a luncheon menu. An unusual tea bread could be the perfect accompaniment to your first course, lunch, or dinner.

Sandwiches

Versatile Vegetarian Sandwich

¼ cup grated cabbage
¼ cup grated carrots
2 tablespoons grated onion
¼ cup finely chopped radishes
½ teaspoon celery seed
Salt, to taste
Pepper, to taste
¼ cup grated sharp Cheddar
¼ cup mayonnaise
8 thin slices whole wheat bread

Mix all vegetables, seasonings, and cheese with mayonnaise and spread on bread slices. Use more mayonnaise, if needed, and other vegetables, if you like. Try this as a roll-up with lavash or pita bread.

YIELD: 4 SANDWICHES

Fresh Herb Sandwich

2 to 3 tablespoons chopped
  herbs
2 teaspoons unsalted butter
2 slices white bread

Select a pleasing combination of herbs, such as equal parts of basil, chives, dill, and parsley. Butter one side of each slice of bread to keep the herbs in place. Spread herbs on one buttered slice and top with the other. Press slices together lightly and cut in half or quarters.

YIELD: 1 SANDWICH

The English tradition of serving fresh herb sandwiches was preserved by the Colonists and remains popular with New England gardeners today. Creative gardeners might add snips of nasturtium leaves and flowers to an herb combination. Basil, chervil, chives, dill, lovage (an old-fashioned herb resembling celery in appearance and taste), rosemary, and savory are equally flavorful. Stronger herbs like fennel, mint, marjoram, sage, tarragon, and thyme should be used in smaller proportion. For example, equal parts of dill and parsley could be combined with a small amount of tarragon.

Seafood, Poultry, Meats

While seafood has long been associated with New England cooking, poultry and meat dishes are traditional as well. Here you will find old favorites that have been updated as well as contemporary recipes to please the most discriminating palates. As decisions about a main course begin to shape your menu, you might consider: Will the entrée be typically American or more European in flavor? Will it have an Asian flair? Are you cooking for a crowd, perhaps serving buffet style, or will your dinner be more intimate? Under any circumstance, personal touches and favorite serving pieces will enhance the presentation of your meal.

Rocking chair, 1975
Made by SAM MALOOF, born 1916

Seafood

When buying fish and shellfish, let your eyes and nose be your guide. Look for moist flesh that glistens but is not slimy. Fresh seafood smells like an ocean breeze, never fishy.

Swordfish Nantucket

Swordfish steak, 1 to 1½ inch thick
1 cup sour cream
Salt, to taste
Paprika, to taste
Citrus Butter (page 153)

Wipe swordfish with a paper towel. Place fish on a rack and broil for 5 minutes. Remove from the oven, turn over, and spread thickly with sour cream. Season with salt and paprika. Place in a preheated 425-degree oven and bake for 20 minutes, or until fish flakes easily when tested with a fork. Serve with citrus butter.

YIELD: 4 SERVINGS

Bluefish with Mustard

3 pounds bluefish fillets
2 tablespoons balsamic vinegar
3 tablespoons coarse-grained mustard
⅓ cup extra virgin olive oil
1 cup dry white wine
Salt, to taste
Pepper, to taste

Rinse the fillets and remove any pin bones from the center. In a bowl, mix balsamic vinegar and mustard; whisk in oil in a thin stream, then wine, salt, and pepper. Lay fillets in a large, deep dish, pour vinegar mixture over, and turn fillets so they are coated on both sides. Cover loosely with foil and refrigerate for at least 1 hour and up to 8 hours. Thoroughly oil the grill rack and position it about 4 inches above the coals. Place fillets on the rack with the skin side up. Broil 4 minutes, turn fillets, and finish skin side down, approximately 4 more minutes, depending on the thickness.

YIELD: 6 SERVINGS

To prevent the flesh from falling into the grill, be sure to finish broiling skin side down.

Cape Cod Bluefish

1½ pounds bluefish fillets
1 tablespoon Dijon mustard
1 teaspoon peeled and minced ginger
½ teaspoon kosher salt
Freshly ground pepper, to taste
1 cup sour cream
1 tablespoon lemon juice
3 tablespoons chopped chives

Rinse and dry fillets and lay them in a lightly buttered baking pan or dish. Mix together mustard, ginger, salt, pepper, sour cream, and lemon juice; spread over fillets. Cover with foil and bake in a preheated 375-degree oven for 10 minutes, or 10 minutes for each inch of thickness as measured at the thickest part of the fillet. Remove foil and place fish under a broiler for about 5 minutes to brown. Garnish with chopped chives.

YIELD: 4 SERVINGS   *A very popular dish on the Islands and Cape Cod.*

Marsh bowl
Egypt, Dynasty 18, 1539–1295/1292 B.C.

Scallops in Wine

2½ pounds sea scallops

1½ cups dry white wine

1 pound carrots, shredded

½ pound snow peas

Salt, to taste

Parsley sprigs

WINE SAUCE

8 scallions, minced

½ cup finely chopped parsley

2 teaspoons salt

1 teaspoon white pepper

1 to 2 tablespoons white
vinegar, to taste

¼ cup water

1 cup dry white wine

Simmer scallops in wine for 5 minutes; remove to a warm platter. Save the liquid, and steam carrots over it for 4 minutes. Steam snow peas separately for 1 to 2 minutes. Place vegetables and scallops on a bed of carrots and encircle with snow peas. Season with salt. Pour sauce over all and garnish with parsley.

To make sauce, cook scallions, parsley, salt, and pepper in vinegar, water, and wine for 3 to 4 minutes, or until liquid reduces slightly.

YIELD: 4 TO 6 SERVINGS

Fresh sea scallops are firm and moist and smell sweet. Their color ranges from pale white to pink-beige with no discernible difference in flavor.

Steamed Mussels with Pancetta

2½ pounds fresh mussels

1 shallot, thinly sliced

¼ cup thyme leaves

6 tablespoons unsalted butter

2 cups dry white wine

8 ounces pancetta, finely
chopped and cooked until
fat is rendered

Kosher salt, to taste

White pepper, to taste

2 cups Crème Fraîche (p. 68)

2 egg yolks

Parsley

Crusty bread

Scrub and debeard mussels. Combine the first 8 ingredients in a large saucepan (8- to 10-inch diameter). Cover tightly and steam over medium heat until mussels open, about 4 to 6 minutes. Stir gently. Remove open mussels, leaving the liquid in the pot and discarding any unopened mussels. Reduce the liquid on high heat to 1 cup. Combine crème fraîche and egg yolks and whisk until smooth; add to the reduced liquid. Return the mussels to the pot and bring to a simmer. Cook down to a velvety sauce and garnish with minced parsley. Serve with a crusty bread for dipping into the sauce.

YIELD: 4 SERVINGS

This dish reheats well, if there is ever any left! Crème fraîche is also available commercially.

Chinese Chili Shrimp

12 large shrimp, shelled and
   deveined
1 tablespoon dry white wine
2 tablespoons vegetable oil
1 tablespoon minced scallion
1 clove garlic, minced
Cilantro sprig or curly parsley

SAUCE

2 teaspoons sugar
½ teaspoon salt
2 teaspoons dry white wine or
   sake
2 teaspoons cornstarch,
   dissolved in 2 teaspoons
   water
2 tablespoons soy sauce
3 tablespoons ketchup
½ teaspoon Chinese chili paste

Combine shrimp and wine and let stand for 10 minutes. Heat oil in a wok or skillet and sauté scallion and garlic for about 2 minutes, or until fragrant. Mix sauce ingredients in a small bowl. Add shrimp to the wok and stir-fry over high heat, until shrimp turns pink. Mix sauce again to incorporate cornstarch and then pour over shrimp. Stir quickly until sauce thickens and coats shrimp. Place on a hot serving platter and garnish with cilantro or parsley.

YIELD: 3 TO 4 SERVINGS

Chinese chili paste can be found in the international foods section of most large supermarkets or in Asian food stores.

Baked Scrod with Crumb Topping

4 (6-ounce) scrod fillets,
   thick (loin) cut
2 teaspoons extra virgin
   olive oil
¼ teaspoon salt
¼ teaspoon coarsely ground
   black pepper
Buttered Fresh Bread Crumbs
   (page 144)
½ teaspoon grated lemon peel
¼ cup loosely packed parsley
   leaves, chopped
Lemon wedges

Rub fish with oil, place in a shallow baking pan, and sprinkle with salt and pepper. Bake in a preheated 450-degree oven for 15 minutes. While the fish bakes, prepare the bread crumbs. When they are golden brown, toss them quickly with lemon peel. Remove fish from the oven, sprinkle with crumb mixture, and return to the oven; bake 5 minutes longer, or until fish turns opaque. Garnish with parsley and serve with lemon wedges.

YIELD: 4 SERVINGS

Simply baked fish is the essence of good New England coastal cookery. Haddock or other firm white fish may be substituted.

Roast Bass with Caramelized Onions

2 large red onions, thinly sliced

2 tablespoons extra virgin
olive oil

2 tablespoons brown sugar

2 tablespoons balsamic vinegar

4 (6- to 8-ounce) bass fillets,
with skin

¼ cup plus 2 tablespoons extra
virgin olive oil, divided

Salt, to taste

Freshly ground black pepper,
to taste

½ cup clam juice or chicken
stock

¼ cup lemon juice

1 tablespoon chopped oregano

½ teaspoon minced garlic

2 tablespoons chopped parsley

To caramelize onions, sauté in olive oil over medium heat for 15 to 20 minutes, or until light brown. Add sugar; cook for 3 minutes. Add vinegar and cook for 1 minute. Spread onions on the bottom of a baking pan. Lay fillets skin side down on the onions and season with 2 tablespoons olive oil, salt, and pepper. Cover tightly with foil and roast in a preheated 400-degree oven for 25 minutes. To prepare the lemon sauce, combine clam juice, lemon juice, oregano, and garlic in a small saucepan and bring to a boil. Cook for 2 to 3 minutes, until reduced to about 5 tablespoons. Strain reduced liquid and pour into a blender. With the motor running on medium speed, slowly add ¼ cup olive oil. Transfer the mixture to a saucepan and season with salt and pepper. Keep warm—not hot—over very low heat. If the sauce separates, return it to the blender and blend at high speed for about 30 seconds. Place fish on serving plates; top with caramelized onions, spoon warm lemon sauce around fish, and sprinkle with parsley.

YIELD: 4 SERVINGS

Poultry

Always buy the freshest chicken available; it should be plump with creamy white to yellowish skin. Check the sell date and look for a package that contains very little or no liquid. For safety reasons, chicken should never be undercooked; on the other hand, overcooking can ruin its texture and flavor. Chicken is best on both counts when it cooks until the juices run clear.

Mediterranean Stuffed Chicken Breasts

½ cup finely chopped red
  onion
2 tablespoons extra virgin
  olive oil, divided
1½ teaspoons minced garlic
½ cup pitted Kalamata olives,
  cut in strips
¼ cup pine nuts, lightly toasted
½ cup sun-dried tomatoes
  packed in oil, drained,
  patted dry, and cut in strips
¼ pound feta, crumbled
2 tablespoons Parmesan
1 tablespoon ground marjoram
Salt, to taste
Pepper, to taste
3 whole boneless, skinless
  chicken breasts, halved
Sun-dried tomatoes

Sauté onions in 1 tablespoon olive oil, stirring until softened. Add garlic and cook 1 minute. Stir in olives, pine nuts, tomatoes, cheeses, marjoram, salt, and pepper. Rinse chicken breasts in cold water and pat dry. Slice a deep pocket into the thicker end of each chicken breast, making it as wide inside as possible. Fill each breast with one-sixth of the filling, using a toothpick to close the pocket. Heat remaining 1 tablespoon olive oil in a clean skillet and brown the tops of the breasts. Place in a baking pan, browned side up, and bake for 12 minutes in a preheated 350-degree oven, or until juices run clear. Remove the toothpicks and garnish with sun-dried tomatoes.

YIELD: 4 SERVINGS

Can be made a day ahead, sliced, and served at room temperature. Save any extra stuffing for another day; stir into hot pasta that has been lightly dressed with extra virgin olive oil.

Marinated Chicken with Spicy Peanut Sauce

MARINADE
½ cup minced onion
¼ cup extra virgin olive oil
¼ cup lemon juice
3 tablespoons soy sauce
2 tablespoons dark rum
1 tablespoon sugar
1 tablespoon peeled and
   minced ginger
3 cloves garlic, minced
1 teaspoon red pepper flakes
1 teaspoon salt

2 whole boneless, skinless
   chicken breasts, halved
Chopped peanuts, chives,
   or parsley

SAUCE
½ cup reserved marinade
3 tablespoons chunky peanut
   butter
½ cup heavy cream

Combine marinade ingredients and blend well. Rinse chicken breasts in cold water, pat dry, and marinate for 2 hours. Remove breasts, reserving ½ cup marinade; use remaining marinade to baste chicken. Grill or broil until juices run clear, about 20 minutes. In a stainless steel or enameled saucepan, bring reserved marinade to a boil, add peanut butter, and cook mixture over low heat, whisking until smooth. Stir in heavy cream, whisking constantly, until smooth and thick. Garnish with chopped peanuts, chives, or parsley.

YIELD: 4 SERVINGS

Serve this savory dish with Roasted Asparagus (page 136) and pineapple rings that have been sprinkled with brown sugar and broiled until warm and bubbling.

Skyphos (two-handled cup) with preparations for a Bacchic sacrifice, Roman, Imperial Period, A.D. 1–30

Country Chicken

6 tablespoons currants

Madeira, to cover

3 whole boneless, skinless
chicken breasts, halved

½ cup flour

I teaspoon salt

I teaspoon black pepper

5 tablespoons extra virgin
olive oil

⅓ cup diced onion

⅓ cup diced green bell pepper

I clove garlic, crushed

1½ teaspoons curry powder

½ teaspoon ground thyme

3½ cups canned plum
tomatoes, chopped and
liquid reserved

¼ cup slivered almonds,
toasted

Warm currants in Madeira and set aside to marinate. Rinse chicken breasts in cold water and pat dry. Place chicken in a plastic bag with flour, salt, and pepper and shake to coat. Heat oil in a skillet, brown both sides of chicken, and remove chicken to a baking pan. Drain currants and sauté with onion, pepper, garlic, curry powder, and thyme. Add tomatoes with their liquid and simmer until hot. Pour over chicken and sprinkle with almonds. Bake in a preheated 350-degree oven for 20 to 30 minutes.

YIELD: 6 SERVINGS

This old Colonial recipe has been updated with contemporary ingredients.

German Chicken

1 (3- to 5-pound) roasting
chicken, giblets removed
1 (15-ounce) can sauerkraut

Rinse chicken in cold water, pat dry, and place in a roasting pan. Drain sauerkraut and put some into the cavity; spread remainder over the breast. Roast in a preheated 350-degree oven for 2 to 2½ hours, or until a thermometer registers 160 to 165 degrees, juices run clear, and the legs move easily.

YIELD: 4 TO 6 SERVINGS

This method produces a very moist chicken, requires no other seasonings, and cuts down on oven spatter. For a complete one-pan dinner, add potato wedges, whole baby carrots, and unpeeled apple slices during the last hour of roasting.

Asian Stuffed Portobello Mushrooms

6 stalks lemongrass

7 scallions, minced

1½ tablespoons plus 1 teaspoon
  sugar

2 tablespoons nam pla (fish
  sauce)

1 pound ground turkey

1 egg, beaten

4 large portobello mushrooms

Cooking oil spray

1 lime

1 teaspoon cornstarch
  dissolved in 2 teaspoons
  water (optional)

Discard outer leaves of lemongrass. Trim about ¾ inch from the bottom of each stalk and several inches of the upper leaves so that 5 to 6 inches of the tender center is left. Pulse stalks in a food processor until finely minced. Combine lemongrass, scallions, sugar, nam pla, ground turkey, and egg in a large bowl; mix thoroughly and set aside. Clean mushrooms and remove stems. Using a small spoon, carefully scrape out gills to create a shallow bowl. Gently fill the cavity of each mushroom with one-quarter of the turkey filling. Place mushrooms, filling side up, on a baking dish lightly sprayed with cooking oil. Bake in a preheated 350-degree oven for 30 minutes. If a darker surface is preferred, place under the broiler for 1 to 2 minutes. Serve with a wedge of lime.

VARIATION: Strain any pan juices that may have collected, and thicken slightly with cornstarch; bring to a boil. Pour over mushrooms.

YIELD: 4 SERVINGS

Cut these mushrooms into bite-size wedges and serve hot or at room temperature as canapés. The turkey stuffing also makes an unusual meat-loaf. Bake in a shallow 8 × 8-inch pan for 30 minutes. For sandwiches, fill with stuffing and spread with the peel and juice of ½ lime mixed into 2 tablespoons mayonnaise. Nam pla can be purchased in the international foods section of most large supermarkets.

Mushrooms netsuke
Japan, early to mid-19th century

Meats

When buying lamb, look for meat that is rosy red with firm waxy fat. It is always best to trim the unpalatable excess fat. Be careful when you cook lamb; its delicate flavor and texture are lost if the meat is overdone.

Mongolian Lamb

MARINADE

1 tablespoon soy sauce

1 tablespoon sugar

1 tablespoon hoisin sauce

1 tablespoon cornstarch

1 teaspoon sesame oil

1 teaspoon sherry

½ teaspoon white pepper

1 small clove garlic, minced

1 pound lamb, boneless loin, rib, or leg

2 tablespoons peanut oil

½ cup walnut pieces, toasted

Chopped cilantro leaves or lemon peel

Rice or noodles

Combine all ingredients for the marinade in a medium bowl. After removing all fat and bone, cut lamb into long strips ½ inch wide. Marinate strips for at least 1 hour, preferably 4 to 5. Heat a large skillet or wok, and add peanut oil. When oil is hot, stir-fry lamb at high heat for 4 to 5 minutes, or until brown. Add walnuts and continue cooking for 30 seconds. Transfer to a heated platter and garnish with cilantro or lemon peel. Serve immediately with rice or noodles.

YIELD: 2 TO 3 SERVINGS

Hoisin, a spicy-sweet Chinese sauce, can be purchased in the international foods section of most large supermarkets.

Butterflied Leg of Lamb

1 cup soy sauce
½ cup rice vinegar
½ cup pineapple juice
½ cup brown sugar
1 garlic clove, crushed
1 (4- to 5-pound) butterflied
   leg of lamb, trimmed of fat
Salt, to taste
Pepper, to taste
Lemon slices or mint leaves
Roast potatoes or rice pilaf

Combine soy sauce, vinegar, pineapple juice, brown sugar, and garlic in a saucepan; bring to a boil and then let cool to room temperature. Place lamb in a large, shallow glass baking pan and pour marinade over meat. Marinate at least 4 hours (or up to 2 days) in the refrigerator, turning the meat occasionally.

Place the rack 4 inches from the heat and grill the lamb slowly, about 10 to 15 minutes on each side, basting frequently with the marinade. Because of the uneven thickness of the meat, some of the lamb will be rare and some medium to well done. The internal temperature in the thickest part should be 125 degrees. Transfer meat to a platter and set on a warm plate for 10 minutes to rest before slicing. Cut meat along its natural lines and slice thinly across the grain. Garnish with lemon slices or bunches of mint leaves. (To cook in the oven, preheat the broiler, place the lamb on the rack of a broiling pan at the closest position to the source of heat, and follow the directions for grilling.) Serve with roast potatoes or rice pilaf.

YIELD: 8 TO 10 SERVINGS

Ask the butcher to bone the leg of lamb and slit the meat lengthwise so that it will spread out flat like a thick steak.

Lamb Shanks with White Beans

6 lamb shanks
6 cloves garlic, unpeeled
4 medium onions, quartered
8 carrots, quartered
Extra virgin olive oil,
    for drizzling
Salt, to taste
Pepper, to taste
8 cups water, divided
6 plum tomatoes, peeled,
    seeded, and chopped
¼ cup chopped oregano
¼ cup chopped rosemary
3 tablespoons black olive
    tapenade

WHITE BEANS
1 pound dried small white
    beans, soaked overnight
    and drained
1 onion, finely chopped
3 plum tomatoes, peeled,
    seeded, and chopped
Handful oregano, chopped
Handful rosemary, chopped
Salt, to taste
Pepper, to taste
Extra oregano and rosemary,
    to garnish

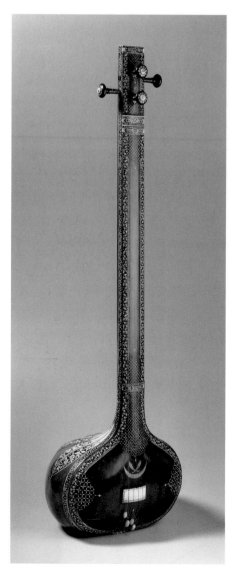

Lute (tambura)
India, 19th century

Divide lamb shanks, garlic, onions, and carrots into 2 large roasting pans to allow enough room for ingredients to brown well. Drizzle with olive oil and season with salt and pepper. Roast in a preheated 450-degree oven for 60 to 70 minutes, or until the onions are burned at the edges and the meat has shrunk from the bone. Reduce heat to 350 degrees. Remove lamb and vegetables from the pans. Press out the garlic pulp and discard the skins. Set one of the pans directly over a burner and turn the heat to high. Carefully pour in 2 cups of water, scraping the bottom of the pan. Remove from the heat and add all the lamb shanks, vegetables, and garlic to the pan. Deglaze the second pan with 2 more cups of water and add the liquid to the first pan. Add the remaining 4 cups water, tomatoes, oregano, rosemary, salt, and pepper. Cover with foil, return to oven, and cook for 1 hour. Remove the foil, turn shanks and vegetables, and continue cooking, uncovered, for 1 hour, or until meat falls off the bone. If refrigerating overnight (see comment below), stop here. If not, stir tapenade into cooking liquid and taste for seasoning.

Prepare the white beans. In a large, heavy pot, combine beans and onion. Add water just to cover. Bring to a boil and lower heat. Add tomatoes, oregano, and rosemary. Cover the pan and simmer for 1½ to 2 hours, until tender, adding more water if beans seem dry. When the lamb is cooked through, ladle about 1 cup of the lamb cooking liquid (preferably with the added tapenade) to the beans. Bring to a boil and simmer the beans, uncovered, for 20 minutes. Add salt, pepper, oregano, and rosemary. Serve with lamb.

YIELD: 6 SERVINGS

Because it is difficult to remove all the fat from lamb shanks, cook them one day; then skim the fat and reheat them the following day. After cooking, separate the meat from the liquid and refrigerate both. Remove all solidified fat. Transfer meat and vegetables to a roasting pan. Add cooking juices, cover with foil, and reheat in a preheated 375-degree oven for 50 minutes, turning meat several times. Add tapenade. Small jars of tapenade are available in larger supermarkets or specialty food stores.

When buying veal, look for meat that is uniformly pinkish to grayish white with no marbling—the whiter the better. This lean, delicate meat should not be overcooked.

Veal Scaloppine with Peppers

1 red bell pepper, seeded
1 yellow bell pepper, seeded
2 scallions, cut in 2-inch
    lengths
1 tablespoon extra virgin
    olive oil
3 tablespoons flour
Salt, to taste
Pepper, to taste
1 pound veal scallops, pounded
    thin
4 tablespoons unsalted butter,
    divided
Peel and juice of 1 large lime
1 cup chicken stock
1½ tablespoons peeled and
    chopped ginger
1 teaspoon coarsely ground
    pepper
Rice, couscous, or quinoa

Slice peppers into thin strips and sauté with scallions in olive oil in a large skillet until tender; remove and set aside. Combine flour, salt, and pepper and dredge veal in mixture. Add 2 tablespoons butter to the skillet. Sauté veal, a few slices at a time, 1 to 2 minutes per side, and remove to a warm platter. Grate lime peel and reserve for garnish. In the skillet, combine stock, lime juice, ginger, and pepper. Heat to boiling and reduce mixture by about one-half. Add remaining 2 tablespoons butter, peppers, and scallions, stirring constantly. Pour sauce over veal. Serve with rice, couscous, or quinoa and garnish with grated lime peel.

YIELD: 4 SERVINGS

Look for thinly sliced veal medallions. This recipe also works well with turkey or chicken cutlets.

THOMAS ROWLANDSON, 1756–1827
The Man of Taste, about 1807

Veal Zurich Style

3 tablespoons minced shallots
1 cup sliced mushrooms
6 tablespoons butter, divided
1½ pounds veal cutlets
2 tablespoons cornstarch
½ teaspoon salt
¼ teaspoon white pepper
1 tablespoon chopped rosemary
   leaves
2 cups dry white wine, heated
½ cup light cream
Chopped parsley
Rosemary sprigs

Sauté shallots and mushrooms in 2 tablespoons butter until golden, about 5 minutes. Remove from the pan and set aside. Pat cutlets dry; sauté quickly in remaining butter, a few slices at a time, until light brown, about 4 minutes each side. Remove veal to a shallow baking dish. When all veal is cooked, top with shallots and mushrooms and keep warm. To the butter remaining in the skillet, add cornstarch, salt, pepper, and rosemary. Gradually stir in wine and boil rapidly to thicken and reduce liquid by one-half. Add cream and heat to warm; pour over veal. Bake in a preheated 350-degree oven 20 to 25 minutes, or until bubbly. Garnish with parsley and rosemary.

YIELD: 4 SERVINGS

Veal Creole

2 tablespoons extra virgin
olive oil
2 pounds boneless veal stew
meat, cut into 1½-inch
cubes
½ cup chopped onion
1 teaspoon salt
Pepper, to taste
½ teaspoon dried thyme leaves
1 cup beef stock
1 cup white wine
½ small (8-ounce) unpeeled
eggplant, cut into 2-inch
strips ½ inch thick
2 large tomatoes (1 pound),
peeled, seeded, and cut into
8 wedges each
1 green bell pepper, seeded
and sliced
1 red bell pepper, seeded
and sliced
2 tablespoons flour
¼ cup cold water
Rice

Heat oil in a large skillet or a 5-quart Dutch oven;
sauté veal, a few pieces at a time, over medium-high
heat until well browned on all sides, about 20 minutes.
Remove the pieces as they brown. To oil remaining in
the skillet, add onion and sauté, stirring until golden,
about 3 minutes. Add salt, pepper, and thyme. Return
veal to the skillet; add beef stock and wine. Bring mixture to a boil, reduce heat, and simmer, covered, for
45 to 60 minutes, or until veal is tender. Meanwhile,
wash and prepare vegetables. Stir flour into water,
mixing until smooth. Add to veal mixture, bring to a
boil, and stir until slightly thickened. Add eggplant
strips and simmer, covered, for 10 to 15 minutes.
Add tomato and peppers and simmer for 10 minutes,
or until peppers are just tender. Serve with rice.

YIELD: 8 SERVINGS

Buy Prime or high-quality Choice grade cuts of beef that are bright red and well marbled. The meat should be finely textured and the fat creamy white with the appearance of freshly cut edges.

Fillet of Beef Tenderloin

MARINADE

¼ cup balsamic vinegar

2 tablespoons lemon juice

1 cup red wine

¼ cup extra virgin olive oil

¼ cup chopped rosemary leaves

2 large cloves garlic, peeled and crushed

Salt, to taste

15 peppercorns, coarsely crushed

1 (3- to 3½-pound) fillet of beef tenderloin, trimmed of fat

Whisk together marinade ingredients. Place fillet in a nonreactive pan with marinade, turning to coat well. Cover with plastic wrap and refrigerate overnight. Grill fillet over hot coals approximately 30 minutes, for medium rare. (For oven preparation, first sear the fillet on all sides in a heavy skillet on top of the stove and then roast it in a preheated 450-degree oven for approximately 20 minutes, or until a meat thermometer registers 130 degrees. The fillet may be roasted 2 days in advance and kept wrapped and chilled.) Serve hot or at room temperature with Red Onion Marmalade (page 152) and Cucumber Horseradish Dressing (page 68).

To serve as an hors d'oeuvre or buffet item, cool to room temperature and carve in ¼-inch slices; serve on toasted French bread that has been brushed with olive oil and spread with cucumber horseradish dressing.

YIELD: 8 SERVINGS AS MAIN COURSE;
20 OR MORE AS HORS D'OEUVRES

Korean Broiled Beef

MARINADE

¼ cup soy sauce

2 tablespoons vegetable oil

1 tablespoon sesame oil

3 tablespoons sugar or less,
   to taste

⅓ cup finely chopped scallions
   (reserve white ends for
   garnish)

⅓ cup finely chopped garlic

¼ teaspoon black pepper

3 tablespoons white sesame
   seeds, toasted until light
   brown

1½ pounds sirloin steak
Rice

Combine soy sauce, oils, sugar, scallions, garlic, and
pepper in a medium bowl or gallon-size resealable plastic bag. Toast sesame seeds in an oven or dry skillet over
low heat until light brown. Add warm sesame seeds to
marinade. Add steak and refrigerate for at least 3 hours
or overnight. Remove steak from marinade, reserving
the liquid, and broil or grill on both sides according
to desired degree of doneness; let it rest for 5 minutes
before slicing against the grain. Heat the marinade
to a boil. Pour pan juices over steak and garnish with
minced scallions. Serve with rice and hot marinade
on the side.

YIELD: 4 SERVINGS

Japanese Grilled Beef

SAUCE

1 cup soy sauce

1 cup water

¾ cup brown sugar

2 teaspoons cider vinegar

2 teaspoons sesame oil

2 teaspoons ginger juice
(yield of about 1-inch section
grated, pulp discarded)

1 tablespoon lime juice

1-inch-wide slice of daikon,
peeled, grated, and gently
squeezed dry

1½ pounds sirloin tips, thinly
sliced against the grain

Any combination of onions,
mushrooms, zucchini, bell
peppers, string beans, eggplant, broccoli, snow peas,
or cabbage, sliced into bite-
size pieces

¼ to ½ cup oil for cooking

Cooked rice

In a medium saucepan, combine soy sauce, water, and brown sugar. Boil for 5 minutes and then add vinegar, oil, juices, and daikon. Remove from heat. (Sauce can be made a few days ahead, refrigerated, and returned to room temperature to serve.) Guests cook their own meal in a shared electric fry pan. Place the fry pan in the center of the table and set each place with a pair of chopsticks or a fondue fork and a dinner fork. Place a bowl of dipping sauce, a bowl of rice, and a plate of steak and vegetables in front of each guest. Heat the electric fry pan to medium and add oil for cooking as needed.

YIELD: 4 SERVINGS

This participatory entrée is entertaining as well as delicious and a good "ice breaker" or enjoyable meal for family and friends. Most of it can be prepared ahead. Since everyone cooks, the host is always part of the activity.

Container in shape of mandarin duck
Vietnam, Le dynasty, late 15th century

Yankee Pot Roast

1 (4- to 6-pound) eye of the
   round roast
1½ teaspoon French Spice Mix
   (page 71)
3 to 4 tablespoons extra virgin
   olive oil
1 cup chopped onions
1 cup sliced mushrooms
2 to 3 teaspoons salt
4 whole cloves
2 bay leaves
2 cups dry red wine
1½ to 2 cups beef stock
2 to 3 cups baby carrots
2 to 3 cups celery pieces,
   1½-inch diagonal cut
6 to 8 medium potatoes,
   peeled and quartered
8 to 10 small white onions
10 to 12 whole mushrooms
Parsley

Rub entire roast with French spice mix; set aside. In a large Dutch oven or roasting pan with a tight lid, heat olive oil over medium-high heat, and add chopped onions and sliced mushrooms; sauté for about 5 minutes until light brown, remove vegetables, and reserve. Add the roast and cook on all sides until dark brown, allowing 15 minutes for a good, rich color. Return onions and mushrooms to the pan; add salt, cloves, bay leaves, wine, and enough beef stock to fill the bottom of pot with ½ to 1 inch of liquid. Cover, reduce heat to very low, and simmer slowly for 3 to 3½ hours, or until meat is tender. (Or roast in a preheated 300-degree oven.) During the last 45 minutes, add carrots, celery, potatoes, small onions, and mushrooms. Transfer roast and vegetables to a large, warm platter. Strain the liquid, return it to the pan, and reduce it to a rich sauce. To serve, slice the meat across the grain and garnish with parsley. Pass the sauce in a gravy boat.

YIELD: 6 TO 10 SERVINGS

A New England version of an American classic! The flavor is enhanced by deeply browning the seasoned meat in oil and then adding a liquid that lends even greater body to the taste. Eye of the round makes an attractive pot roast; a boneless rump or chuck of beef, rolled and tied, is also delicious.

New England Boiled Dinner

1 (4- to 5-pound) gray, thin-cut corned beef brisket

Cold water, to cover

2 onions, peeled and quartered

6 to 10 black peppercorns, to taste

4 whole cloves

2 bay leaves

½ teaspoon paprika

6 carrots, peeled and cut into 3-inch pieces

4 celery ribs, cut into 3-inch pieces

5 potatoes, peeled and quartered

10 to 12 pearl onions, peeled

3 parsnips, peeled and cut into 3-inch pieces

3 turnips, peeled and quartered

1 head green cabbage, cut into 8 to 10 wedges

10 small beets, peeled (optional)

Parsley sprigs for garnish

Horseradish

Mustards

Rinse meat under running water to remove the surface brine. Place brisket in a large, heavy pot, add cold water to cover, and slowly bring to a boil. Boil 5 minutes, skim the top, add seasonings, and simmer, covered, over low heat about 1 hour per pound, or until tender. (Test the center with a large fork; tines will slip in and out of the meat easily when it is done. The meat shrinks a great deal.) Add water as necessary to keep the brisket covered and occasionally skim off the fat. During the last 45 minutes, add carrots, celery, potatoes, onions, parsnips, and turnips; simmer. Add cabbage wedges and simmer with the other vegetables for the last 7 to 10 minutes. If you choose to serve beets, boil them for 30 to 40 minutes in a separate pot, so as not to color the other vegetables. Turn off the heat and let the meat rest in the broth a few minutes to absorb the juices. Cut into thin slices at a slight angle, always across the grain. Serve cabbage and beets in separate dishes and arrange remaining vegetables on a large, deep platter with the meat. Garnish with parsley. Serve with horseradish or a variety of mustards and provide additional hot stock in a gravy boat.

YIELD: 8 TO 10 SERVINGS

This celebrated New England dinner has survived more than 200 years of culinary cold-weather tradition. It is still prepared with all the customary vegetables. Leftover corned beef makes delicious sandwiches. A cured pork shoulder, while unconventional, also makes a flavorful meal.

Pinwheel Meatloaf

4 sweet Italian sausages
3 pounds lean ground beef
2 eggs
2 tablespoons tomato paste
I tablespoon Dijon mustard
I tablespoon Worcestershire
    sauce
2 teaspoons salt
I teaspoon pepper
I teaspoon dried basil
I teaspoon dried oregano
2 cups diced red bell peppers
I cup finely chopped onion
2 cups coarsely grated sharp
    Cheddar
2 cups chopped pitted black
    olives
I cup coarsely chopped parsley
Additional parsley sprigs

Prick sausages with a fork and place them in a skillet. Cover sausages with water, bring to a boil, reduce heat, and simmer for 20 minutes. Drain and discard liquid. Return sausages to skillet and brown lightly over medium heat; set aside. In a large bowl, combine ground beef, eggs, tomato paste, mustard, Worcestershire sauce, salt, pepper, basil, and oregano.

Place meat on a large sheet of foil and shape it into a 12 × 15-inch rectangle. Allowing a I-inch outer margin, spread red peppers evenly over the meat surface; follow with onion, and press lightly into the meat. Cover evenly with grated cheese, then olives, and then parsley; press all into place.

Arrange the reserved sausages in a line along one of the long ends of the rectangle. Beginning from the sausage end, roll meat mixture, jellyroll style, lifting the foil to roll meat carefully into a firm pinwheel. Use a long metal spatula to loosen meat from the foil. Pinch the seam closed and place in a shallow baking pan, seam side down. Pinch the ends of the roll to seal, so that cheese will not ooze out. Bake in a preheated 350-degree oven for I hour and IO minutes. With two long spatulas, carefully remove meatloaf to a serving platter. Let rest I5 minutes before slicing, so that the filling holds its decorative pattern. Garnish with parsley sprigs.

YIELD: 10 TO 12 SERVINGS

This special meatloaf is a wonderful buffet entrée or may be served at room temperature for an informal picnic.

Hamburgers with Blue Cheese

½ cup crumbled blue cheese
¼ cup butter
3 pounds ground chuck
Herb Salt (page 70), to taste
Pepper, to taste
¾ cup flour, for dredging

GRILLED GARLIC TOASTS
16 thick slices French bread,
  sliced on diagonal
Extra virgin olive oil
2 cloves garlic, halved crosswise

With the back of a fork or in a food processor, combine blue cheese and butter. On a sheet of foil, shape mixture into a log and freeze for at least 20 minutes, until firm. Divide meat into 8 patties, making a depression in each. Place one-eighth of the butter/cheese mixture in each depression, and form the meat around the filling into 1-inch-thick patties. Season with herb salt and pepper. Lightly dredge patties in flour, covering all sides. Grill to medium rare, about 6 minutes per side. Serve on grilled garlic toasts.

While the hamburgers are grilling, place bread slices around the perimeter of the coals. Grill until golden, about 1 to 2 minutes per side. Remove from the grill, brush on one side with olive oil, and rub with the cut side of garlic.

YIELD: 8 SERVINGS

Vessel in the form of a hare
Near Eastern, Syrian, Neolithic Period,
about 6400–5900 B.C.

Buy pork that is pale pink and firm to the touch. With today's leaner pork, it is important to sear the meat so that it will retain its natural juices.

Fruited Pork Tenderloin

2 (1½-pound) boneless pork
    tenderloins
¼ cup extra virgin olive oil,
    divided
Kosher salt

MARINADE
1½ cups port
1 cup orange juice
3 tablespoons honey
3 tablespoons cider vinegar
3 shallots, minced
3 cloves garlic, minced
½ to 1 cup dried apricots
16 prunes, pitted
2 tablespoons chopped
    rosemary leaves (optional)
Salt, to taste
Pepper, to taste

Rub tenderloins with 2 tablespoons olive oil and salt, and place them in a pan or dish deep enough for marinating. Put marinade ingredients in a saucepan and simmer 5 minutes. Pour warm marinade over pork and cool to room temperature. Cover pork and continue to marinate in the refrigerator at least 4 hours, turning occasionally. Prepare the grill. Remove tenderloins from marinade and sear on both sides until brown; cover the grill and cook 30 to 40 minutes. Pork can also be roasted in a preheated 475-degree oven for about 25 minutes, or until a meat thermometer registers 145 degrees. Boil marinade in a saucepan for 2 minutes. Cut pork into ½-inch slices and spoon marinade over.

YIELD: 6 TO 8 SERVINGS

KAIGETSUDO ANDO, 1671–1743
Watermelon Slicer (detail)

Asian Pork Tenderloin

MARINADE

¼ cup soy sauce

2 tablespoons sesame oil

2 tablespoons brown sugar

½ teaspoon honey

1 tablespoon dry sherry

4 cloves garlic, peeled and
minced

2 tablespoons sesame seeds,
toasted

3 to 4 scallions, sliced on
a diagonal

1½ pounds pork tenderloin

Combine marinade ingredients; add pork, cover, and marinate overnight in the refrigerator. Discard marinade. Grill pork over medium-hot coals, turning occasionally, for 15 to 20 minutes, or until a meat thermometer reaches 155 degrees. Remove pork from the grill and carve into medallions.

YIELD: 4 SERVINGS

Crown Roast of Pork

1 (7- to 9-pound) crown roast
    of pork or 14 to 16 rib chops
3 tablespoons flour
2 teaspoons salt
1 teaspoon pepper
1 teaspoon ground sage
1 tablespoon thyme leaves
½ teaspoon poultry seasoning
½ teaspoon ground cardamom
3 to 4 cups chicken stock,
    divided
½ cup dry Marsala
Thyme sprigs
Bunches of sage
Paper frills

Remove pork from refrigerator ½ hour before cooking. In a small bowl, combine flour, salt, pepper, sage, thyme, poultry seasoning, and cardamom. Rub flour mixture over the entire surface of roast, and place it in an open roasting pan fitted with a rack. Pour 3 cups of chicken stock into the pan, and then roast meat in the bottom third of a preheated 450-degree oven for 30 minutes. Lower temperature to 325 degrees and continue cooking for about 3 hours, or until a meat thermometer, inserted between two ribs in the thickest part of meat, registers 155 to 160 degrees (a total of 25 to 30 minutes per pound). Baste roast occasionally with the pan juices and add up to 1 more cup of chicken stock as needed. Remove roast from the oven, transfer to a large serving platter, cover loosely with aluminum foil, and let stand in a warm place about 15 minutes for easier carving. Skim off the fat, strain the pan juices into a small saucepan, and add Marsala. Bring to a boil and cook for 5 to 10 minutes to concentrate the flavor. Serve alongside the roast. Fill the center with fresh thyme and sage. Decorate the tops of the bones with paper frills. To serve, slice downward on both sides of the rib bone of each chop.

YIELD: 7 TO 8 SERVINGS, 2 CHOPS EACH

Have the butcher shape the crown roast and crack rib chops for easy carving. If desired, bones may be "frenched" by trimming and cleaning the top 2 inches of the rib bones of all excess meat and fat.

Chinese Baby Back Ribs

MARINADE
2 tablespoons peeled and
   minced ginger
I tablespoon minced garlic
I½ cups ketchup
I½ cups soy sauce
½ cup honey
⅓ cup dry sherry
2 tablespoons chopped cilantro

4 to 5 pounds baby back pork
   spareribs
2 tablespoons chopped scallions

Arrange ribs in a large baking dish. Combine marinade ingredients in a small bowl. Mix thoroughly and pour over ribs. Loosely cover and refrigerate overnight. Place a rack in a roasting pan and lay the ribs on top. Pour the marinade over and bake ribs in a preheated 400-degree oven for I¼ hours, basting frequently. Garnish with chopped scallions.

YIELD: 6 SERVINGS

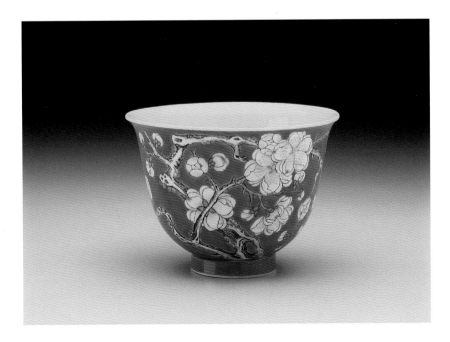

Wine cup
China, Qing dynasty, Kangxi period,
early 18th century

Stuffed Red Peppers

3 tablespoons extra virgin
  olive oil
4 shallots, minced
4 garlic cloves, minced
1½ pounds sweet Italian
  sausage, casings removed
¼ pound mushrooms, coarsely
  chopped
1 tablespoon Dijon mustard
¼ teaspoon Tabasco sauce
1 tablespoon Worcestershire
  sauce
½ cup chopped parsley
1 tablespoon chopped oregano
1 tablespoon chopped rosemary
  leaves
1 tablespoon chopped sage
1 tablespoon chopped thyme
⅛ teaspoon nutmeg
½ cup dry Marsala
1 (8-ounce) can tomato sauce
Grated peel of 1 lemon
Salt, to taste
Pepper, to taste
4 large red bell peppers,
  tops cut off and reserved,
  ribs and seeds removed
Parmesan curls

In a large, heavy skillet, heat oil and cook shallots and garlic until soft. Add sausage, stirring to break up the lumps, and cook until no longer pink. Pour off fat and add mushrooms, mustard, Tabasco and Worcestershire sauces, the herbs, nutmeg, Marsala, tomato sauce, and lemon peel. Simmer about 10 minutes and season with salt and pepper. Let mixture cool. Arrange peppers in a baking dish just large enough to hold them. (Crumple foil to keep peppers upright, if necessary.) Pack mixture tightly into peppers. Cover with the tops and bake in the middle of a preheated 350-degree oven for 45 minutes. Serve with Parmesan curls.

YIELD: 4 SERVINGS

Soft turkey sausage can be used instead of Italian sausage. The stuffing can be made in advance and the peppers filled just before baking. Use a vegetable peeler to make Parmesan curls. This dish goes well with Baked Semolina Gnocchi (page 145), Potato Pancakes with Scallions and Prosciutto (page 143), or Potato Puff (page 143).

HENRY SARGENT, 1770–1845
The Dinner Party, about 1821

Casseroles,
Pastas,
Quiches

A creative combination of foods presented with flair is always appealing. Your main course for a midday meal or informal supper may be a hearty casserole, pasta with a piquant sauce, or a savory quiche. Many of these dishes are easy to prepare and can sometimes be made in advance. Presentation in imaginative, even whimsical, serving pieces will make simple occasions memorable.

Side chairs, 1987
Made by PETER DEAN, born 1951

Casseroles

Moussaka

MEAT SAUCE
2 tablespoons extra virgin
    olive oil
1 cup finely chopped onion
1½ pounds extra lean ground
    lamb, beef, or turkey
1 clove garlic, minced
1 teaspoon dried basil
½ teaspoon dried oregano
½ teaspoon cinnamon
½ teaspoon salt
⅛ teaspoon pepper
2 (8-ounce) cans tomato sauce

YOGURT SAUCE
3 eggs
1 tablespoon flour
2 cups plain nonfat yogurt
½ teaspoon salt
⅛ teaspoon white pepper
⅛ teaspoon nutmeg

2 (1-pound) eggplants
Cooking spray or extra virgin
    olive oil
½ cup grated Cheddar, divided
½ cup grated Parmesan,
    divided
¼ cup dried bread crumbs,
    divided

To make meat sauce, heat oil in large skillet and sauté onion, meat, and garlic, stirring until brown. Skim off fat. Add herbs, spices, and tomato sauce; simmer, uncovered, for ½ hour. For yogurt sauce, beat eggs with a whisk in a 1½-quart pan. Blend in flour and yogurt. Add seasonings. Cook over medium-low heat, stirring frequently, until mixture comes to a boil and thickens, 6 to 8 minutes.

Slice unpeeled eggplants lengthwise into ½-inch-thick pieces. Spray or brush lightly with oil. Broil until golden brown on both sides. Layer half the eggplant slices in a 13 × 9 × 2-inch greased baking dish. Sprinkle with 2 tablespoons each Cheddar and Parmesan. Stir 2 tablespoons bread crumbs into meat sauce and spoon evenly onto casserole. Sprinkle 2 tablespoons each of Cheddar and Parmesan over meat sauce. Arrange remaining eggplant slices on top. Pour yogurt sauce over and sprinkle with remaining cheese and bread crumbs. Bake in a preheated 350-degree oven for 40 to 45 minutes, until top is golden and puffed (or freeze and then thaw to room temperature before baking). After removing moussaka from the oven, let it stand for 10 minutes before cutting into squares.

YIELD: 6 TO 8 SERVINGS

Serve with rice, tossed salad, and crusty French bread. This casserole is great to have in the freezer for entertaining on short notice.

West Indian Curry

3 whole boneless, skinless
   chicken breasts
½ to I cup water
¼ cup butter
I clove garlic, crushed
I onion, chopped
3 ribs celery, chopped
I green bell pepper, seeded
   and chopped
I carrot, scraped and chopped
2 tomatoes, seeded and diced
I Granny Smith or other tart
   apple, seeded and chopped
I tablespoon chopped parsley
I bay leaf
2 whole cloves
⅛ teaspoon ground thyme
⅛ teaspoon ground marjoram
⅛ teaspoon dried mint
¼ teaspoon dried basil
2 tablespoons flour
2 tablespoons curry powder
½ teaspoon salt
½ teaspoon pepper
¼ teaspoon cayenne
¼ teaspoon nutmeg
2 cups chicken stock
I cup dry white wine
Rice
Accompaniments for Curry
   (page 152)

Place chicken in water and bring to a boil; reduce heat and simmer, covered, until tender or the juices run clear, about 10 minutes. Cool and cut into 1-inch cubes. Melt butter in a skillet. Add garlic, chopped vegetables and apple, parsley, bay leaf, cloves, thyme, marjoram, mint, and basil. Cook until vegetables are tender, about 20 minutes. Sprinkle with flour and curry powder, salt, pepper, cayenne, and nutmeg; mix well. Cook, stirring, for 5 minutes. Add stock. (Can be prepared in advance up to this point.) When mixture begins to thicken, add wine. Add chicken and cook slowly for ½ hour. Remove bay leaf and cloves. Serve with rice and accompaniments for curry.

VARIATION: Instead of chicken, cook 1¼ pounds shrimp for 3 minutes; cool, set aside, and add during the last few minutes of cooking to reheat.

YIELD: 4 TO 6 SERVINGS

Risotto with Spicy Sausage and Mushrooms

3 hot Italian sausages

2 large zucchini, quartered
  lengthwise and seeded

3 tablespoons extra virgin olive
  oil, divided

½ pound fresh shiitake mushrooms, stems removed, caps
  thinly sliced

1 Spanish or Bermuda onion,
  finely chopped

2 cups short-grain rice, preferably Arborio or Carnaroli

Salt, to taste

Freshly ground pepper, to taste

5 cups chicken stock, heated
  to boiling

2 teaspoons chopped rosemary

½ cup freshly grated Parmesan,
  preferably Reggiano

Prick sausages all over with a fork. In a heavy saucepan, cook sausages over medium-high heat, turning often, until golden brown; remove from pan, let cool, and then slice thinly on the diagonal and set aside. Thinly slice zucchini spears crosswise and set aside. In a large, heavy saucepan, heat 1 tablespoon olive oil and sauté mushrooms over medium heat for about 5 minutes or until golden; remove from the pan and set aside. In remaining olive oil, sauté onion over low heat for 8 minutes. Add rice and cook, stirring, for 1 minute. Add mushrooms, zucchini, salt, and pepper, and cook for 1 minute. Stir in stock, ½ cup at a time, and continue cooking, stirring constantly, until rice is creamy and tender but grains remain separate and slightly firm. Add rosemary, cheese, and reserved sausages. Taste for seasoning. Divide risotto among 6 warm, shallow plates and serve at once.

YIELD: 6 SERVINGS

Risotto can be prepared just before company arrives by holding back 1 cup of liquid and then adding it as you reheat.

Smoked Salmon and Spinach Risotto

2 tablespoons unsalted butter, divided

¼ medium onion, chopped

2 cups short-grain rice, preferably Arborio or Carnaroli

1 cup dry white wine

2¾ cups chicken stock

10 to 12 ounces fresh baby or salad spinach, large stems removed, julienned

¼ cup minced chives, divided

6 ounces smoked salmon, sliced thinly crosswise

¾ cup mascarpone cheese (6 ounces)

Salt, to taste

Pepper, to taste

2 ounces Tobiko (Japanese flying fish roe) or golden caviar

Heat 1 tablespoon butter in a heavy 6-quart pot over medium heat. Add onion and cook until wilted but not brown, about 3 minutes. Add rice and stir well for about 30 seconds. Add wine and stir. Add 1 cup stock, turn up the heat, and bring to a boil. Lower the heat to a simmer, and stir mixture with a wooden spoon every minute or so. When rice becomes dry, add another cup of stock. Rice should be covered with a film of stock throughout cooking. Repeat until all stock is added, about 13 minutes. Add spinach, half the chives, and salmon. Mix and cook another 3 to 4 minutes, stirring constantly so that rice does not stick. Remove from the heat and stir in cheese and remaining butter. Season with salt and pepper. Transfer risotto to warm plates and sprinkle with Tobiko and remaining chives. Serve immediately.

YIELD: 4 SERVINGS AS MAIN COURSE,
8 AS FIRST COURSE

You can prepare risotto just before company arrives by holding back 1 cup of liquid and then adding spinach, salmon, and reserved liquid as you reheat it.

Pastas

Greek-Style Shrimp with Pasta

5 tablespoons extra virgin olive oil, divided

I teaspoon minced garlic

2 cups seeded, cubed fresh tomatoes

½ cup dry white wine

Salt, to taste

Pepper, to taste

¼ cup finely chopped basil

I teaspoon dried oregano

1½ pounds medium shrimp, peeled and deveined

⅛ teaspoon red pepper flakes

½ pound feta, crumbled

½ pound pasta

Heat 2 tablespoons olive oil in large skillet and sauté garlic briefly. Add tomatoes and cook about I minute. Add wine, salt, pepper, basil, and oregano, cooking over moderate heat about 10 minutes. Set aside. Sprinkle shrimp with salt and pepper. Heat 3 tablespoons oil in another large skillet, add shrimp, and cook quickly, about I minute, until shrimp just turn pink. Stir as shrimp cool; then sprinkle with red pepper flakes. Spoon shrimp and pan juices into a small baking pan, sprinkle with crumbled feta, and cover with tomato sauce. Bake in a preheated 400-degree oven for 10 minutes, until piping hot. While shrimp are baking, cook pasta al dente and drain; top with shrimp.

YIELD: 4 SERVINGS   *For variety, serve with rice pilaf instead of pasta.*

Linguine with Seared Shrimp

3 cloves garlic
1-inch section ginger, peeled
1 cup coarsely chopped, loosely
    packed cilantro
¼ cup lemon juice
2 tablespoons soy sauce
½ teaspoon extra virgin
    olive oil
2 pounds shrimp, peeled
    and deveined
¾ cup Pesto Genovese
    (page 154)
¼ to ½ cup pasta cooking
    water or chicken stock
1 pound linguine, cooked
    al dente

In a food processor or blender, purée garlic, ginger, and cilantro. Add lemon juice, soy sauce, and olive oil. Toss mixture and shrimp in a medium bowl and refrigerate for 30 minutes, or up to 24 hours. Remove shrimp from marinade and drain well. Heat a large nonstick skillet over high heat until water dropped into it sizzles. Place shrimp in an uncrowded single layer in the skillet and cook for about 1 minute on each side; remove from the pan and set aside. In a small saucepan, heat pesto and liquid. Add to pasta and toss well. Place pasta on a large serving platter and arrange shrimp on top.

YIELD: 4 SERVINGS

Asparagus Linguine with Herb Brown Butter

2 pounds asparagus, stalks
    trimmed and cut in thirds
1 pound linguine
6 tablespoons butter
Cracked black pepper, to taste
2 tablespoons chopped sage
2 tablespoons chopped oregano
2 tablespoons chopped
    marjoram
1 tablespoon lemon juice
Shavings of Reggiano Parmesan

Cook asparagus until tender and drain well. Cook linguine al dente. Drain well, but do not rinse. While pasta is cooking, heat butter, pepper, and herbs in a saucepan over medium heat for 4 to 6 minutes, until butter is golden brown. Lower heat and add lemon juice. Divide pasta into serving bowls, place asparagus on pasta, and spoon herb butter sauce over both. Top with Parmesan.

YIELD: 4 TO 6 SERVINGS

Orecchiette with Broccoflower

5 tablespoons extra virgin olive oil, divided
1 cup Fresh Bread Crumbs (page 144)
½ cup coarsely chopped sun-dried tomatoes packed in oil, and ¼ cup oil
1 large head broccoflower, or 1 bunch broccoli
2 large garlic cloves, chopped
Salt, to taste
Pepper, to taste
¾ pound orecchiette
Grated Reggiano Parmesan

In a 5-quart kettle, bring 4 quarts salted water to a boil for broccoflower and pasta. In a deep, heavy skillet, warm 1½ tablespoons olive oil over medium heat, and gently cook bread crumbs, stirring constantly, until golden. Transfer bread crumbs to a bowl and wipe the skillet clean. Warm sun-dried tomatoes and their oil in the skillet. Add broccoflower to boiling water and cook for 2 to 3 minutes, until tender; remove with a slotted spoon and drain well in a colander, keeping water at a boil. Add broccoflower, chopped garlic, and salt to sun-dried tomatoes and sauté until vegetables take on a pale golden hue, about 3 minutes; keep warm. Cook orecchiette al dente, and drain well. Add pasta, the remaining 3½ tablespoons oil, salt, and pepper to vegetables and toss until well combined. Sprinkle with bread crumbs and freshly grated Parmesan.

YIELD: 4 SERVINGS, AS FIRST COURSE

Ewer
Iran, Ilkhanid, about 1220–30

Baked Rotini with Sausage and Feta

I pound hot Italian sausage,
  casing removed
I cup chopped onion
4 large cloves garlic, minced
I large green or red bell
  pepper, seeded and chopped
½ cup finely chopped sun-
  dried tomatoes packed in
  oil, and 2 tablespoons oil
3½ cups canned crushed
  tomatoes, undrained
I (6-ounce) can tomato paste
½ cup dry red wine
½ cup pitted, chopped
  Kalamata olives
I bay leaf
I tablespoon chopped rosemary
  leaves
I teaspoon fennel seeds
Kosher or sea salt, to taste
Freshly ground pepper, to taste
I pound rotini, cooked al dente
3 medium zucchini, sliced
  ¼ inch thick
½ pound feta, crumbled
½ pound part-skim mozzarella,
  coarsely grated
I cup freshly grated Parmesan
½ cup chopped parsley
  (optional)
Lemon wedges (optional)

Cook sausage, onion, garlic, and bell pepper in a large skillet over medium heat, stirring, for 5 to 10 minutes, until meat is brown and crumbled and onion is soft. Add sun-dried tomatoes and their oil, crushed tomatoes and their liquid, tomato paste, wine, olives, bay leaf, rosemary, fennel, salt, and pepper. Simmer over low heat for 20 minutes. Discard bay leaf. Grease a 13 × 9 × 2-inch baking pan. Spread half the rotini over the bottom of the pan and cover with half the zucchini. Pour half the sauce over zucchini and top with half the feta and half the mozzarella. Repeat the layering, beginning with rotini and ending with cheese. Top with Parmesan and parsley. Cover and bake in the middle of a preheated 350-degree oven for 40 minutes. Remove the cover; place the pan about 6 inches beneath broiler. Broil about 5 minutes, or until Parmesan is nicely brown and mozzarella is bubbling. Garnish with lemon wedges.

YIELD: 8 SERVINGS

Quiches

Savory Cheese Tart

1 pound Monterey Jack, cubed

1 (8-ounce) package cream
    cheese, cubed

8 ounces cottage cheese

6 tablespoons butter

6 eggs, beaten

1 cup milk

2 teaspoons sugar

½ teaspoon sweet Hungarian
    paprika, divided

1 teaspoon salt

½ cup flour

1 teaspoon baking powder

In a food processor, mix cheeses, butter, eggs, milk, sugar, ¼ teaspoon paprika, and salt. Add flour and baking powder and pulse until mixture has just blended. Pour into a greased 14 × 10 × 2-inch baking dish, sprinkle with remaining paprika, and bake in a preheated 350-degree oven for 40 minutes, or until a knife inserted in the center comes out clean.

YIELD: 8 TO 10 SERVINGS

A splendid cheese tart is versatile enough for fancy or informal fare. This version is crustless, and its texture is between that of a quiche and a soufflé.

Soufflé Sandwich with Crabmeat

12 slices firm, white sandwich
    bread, buttered and crusts
    removed

12 slices Swiss

5 eggs

3 cups milk

1 teaspoon Dijon mustard

1 teaspoon salt

1 pound fresh crabmeat,
    shredded

Freshly grated Parmesan

Watercress sprigs

Butter a 13 × 9 × 2-inch baking dish and place half the bread slices, buttered side down, on the bottom. Top each bread slice with 2 slices of Swiss and sprinkle crabmeat on top. Put remaining 6 slices of bread, buttered side up, on top of crabmeat. Beat together eggs, milk, mustard, and salt and pour mixture over all. Refrigerate overnight or at least 8 hours. Bake for ½ hour in a preheated 325-degree oven. Top generously with Parmesan and continue baking for another ½ hour. Cut carefully and remove sandwiches with a spatula. Garnish with watercress.

YIELD: 6 SERVINGS

Smoked Salmon and Dill Quesadilla

½ cup sour cream or Crème
    Fraîche (page 68)
¼ cup chopped dill, divided
Salt, to taste
Pepper, to taste
3 (6-inch) flour tortillas
I cup grated sharp Cheddar
I cup grated Monterey Jack
2 tablespoons chopped red
    onion
8 thin slices smoked salmon
4 teaspoons salmon caviar

In a small bowl, stir together sour cream and 2 table-spoons dill. Add salt and pepper and mix again. Place 2 tortillas on an *ungreased* baking pan. Sprinkle each with cheeses, onion, and remaining dill. Stack one tortilla on top of the other and cover with the remaining tortilla. Bake in a preheated 450-degree oven for 8 to 12 minutes, until tortillas are slightly crisp and cheese has melted. Cut the quesadilla in eighths. Garnish each eighth with smoked salmon, sour cream mixture, and salmon caviar.

YIELD: 8 SERVINGS

Eggplant "Sandwiches"

I (I- to I¼-pound) firm
    eggplant, unpeeled
I½ ounces thinly sliced
    prosciutto
2 to 2½ ounces thinly sliced
    provolone
2 eggs
½ cup fine, dry bread crumbs
½ cup grated Parmesan
2 tablespoons minced parsley
Olive oil spray

Be careful not to lose the idea and charm of this extraordinary little "sandwich" by putting in too much filling. These are good hot or at room temperature.

Slice eggplant crosswise into 14 rounds about ⅜ inch thick. Trim prosciutto to fit in a single layer over each of 7 eggplant rounds. Trim provolone, placing it over prosciutto. Top each "sandwich" with another slice of eggplant and press down to secure fillings. Beat eggs in a shallow dish, and mix together bread crumbs, grated Parmesan, and parsley in another. Dip sandwiches first into beaten egg, coating them evenly and well, and then into crumb mixture, being certain to blanket the edges of the sandwiches as well as the tops and bottoms. Spray a baking pan with olive oil. Arrange sandwiches in the pan and spray with olive oil. Bake in a preheated 375-degree oven, turning once, for 30 minutes or until golden brown. Serve as sandwiches or cut into bite-size pieces.

YIELD: 2 TO 3 SERVINGS AS LUNCHEON, 7 AS FIRST COURSE, OR ABOUT 40 AS HORS D'OEUVRES

Vegetables, Grains, Condiments

This may be just the right time to use
Grandmother's cherished sauceboat or your
newest contemporary bowl. Nothing is too fine
to show off fresh vegetables or exotic grain dishes.
A creative setting might include individual pots
for Boston Baked Beans or a favorite platter with
an arrangement of colorful vegetables. Serve
sauces and condiments to add accent and zest
to all your meals.

Side chair, 1989
Made by KRISTINA MADSEN, born 1955

Vegetables

Spinach Cabrini

1 pound penne
1 pound mushrooms, sliced
1 large onion, chopped (about
    1 cup)
¼ cup butter, melted
3 (10-ounce) packages frozen,
    chopped spinach, thawed
    and drained
4 cups shredded Monterey Jack
2 cups sour cream
½ teaspoon salt
¼ teaspoon pepper
¼ teaspoon dried oregano

Cook pasta al dente and drain. Sauté mushrooms and onion in butter. In a large bowl, stir together all ingredients. Place mixture in a lightly greased 15 × 10 × 2-inch baking dish and bake, uncovered, in a 350-degree oven for 45 minutes.

YIELD: 8 TO 10 SERVINGS

This makes an excellent vegetarian main course or buffet selection.

Mint-Marinated Grilled Red Onions

3 red onions, each cut cross-
    wise into ½-inch slices
¼ cup torn mint leaves
2 tablespoons chopped oregano
½ teaspoon salt
1 teaspoon sugar
¼ cup white vinegar
2 tablespoons extra virgin
    olive oil
Additional oil for brushing
    onions
Pepper, to taste

In a shallow, nonreactive baking pan large enough to hold onion slices in one layer, whisk together mint, oregano, salt, sugar, vinegar, and oil. Add onion slices and marinate, turning occasionally, for at least 3 hours, or refrigerate overnight. Remove onions from marinade and brush with oil. Place small side down on an oiled rack over glowing coals and grill for 8 to 10 minutes, turning once, until onions are translucent. Season with pepper.

YIELD: 4 SERVINGS

Ribbed bowl
Roman, Imperial Period, late
1st century B.C. to 1st century A.D.

Roasted Caramelized Onions

1 large red onion, peeled,
    with root intact
2 large Spanish or Bermuda
    onions, peeled, with roots
    intact
2 tablespoons extra virgin
    olive oil
2 tablespoons Dijon mustard
6 tablespoons chopped thyme,
    divided
Salt, to taste
Freshly ground pepper, to taste
3 tablespoons balsamic vinegar

Cut each onion into 6 or 8 wedges, keeping some root on each piece to hold the layers together. In a bowl, mix together oil, mustard, 3 tablespoons thyme, salt, and pepper. Add onions and toss gently to coat. In a foil-lined baking pan large enough to hold all the onions in one layer, arrange the wedges tightly together, rounded sides down. Sprinkle with vinegar. Cover with foil and roast onions in a preheated 400-degree oven for 45 minutes; remove the foil and continue roasting for 30 minutes, or until onions are golden brown and very tender and the tips are almost burned. Trim off excess root ends after baking. Sprinkle with remaining thyme.

YIELD: 4 SERVINGS

Try this recipe with a variety of onions—Vidalia, red, whole shallots, and whole cippollini. Roasted onions will keep for a week in the refrigerator and reheat well.

Roasted Asparagus

2½ pounds asparagus, trimmed
Olive oil spray
½ cup chopped scallions
2 tablespoons sesame seeds,
   lightly toasted
1 teaspoon kosher or sea salt
1½ tablespoons extra virgin
   olive oil
Lemon juice, to taste

Lightly spray a 15 × 10 × 1-inch jellyroll pan with olive oil. Spread asparagus in one layer and sprinkle with scallions, sesame seeds, salt, and olive oil. Roast in a preheated 500-degree oven for 5 to 10 minutes, depending on the thickness of asparagus. Sprinkle with lemon juice.

Cumin seeds may be substituted for black or white sesame seeds. For an attractive presentation, roast quartered tomatoes with asparagus and arrange on a serving platter.

Marinated Broccoli

3 large bunches broccoli
1 cup cider vinegar
1 tablespoon sugar
1 tablespoon dried dill
1 teaspoon salt
1 teaspoon pepper
1 teaspoon garlic salt
1 cup vegetable oil

Wash and trim broccoli florets into bite-size pieces; discard stems. Combine all other ingredients and pour over broccoli. Refrigerate overnight or for several hours. Drain before serving.

VARIATIONS: After draining broccoli, stir in ¼ cup dried cherries or golden raisins and garnish with lightly toasted pine nuts. Or substitute ¼ cup walnut oil for an equal amount of vegetable oil and, after draining broccoli, stir in ½ cup walnuts.

YIELD: 7 TO 8 CUPS   *Excellent for a buffet. The broccoli adds a bright green touch and a tangy, refreshing taste.*

Roasted Bell Peppers with Walnuts

6 red bell peppers, cut in thirds lengthwise, seeded, and ribs removed

2 tablespoons extra virgin olive oil

1 (14½-ounce) can diced tomatoes, drained (about 1½ cups)

4 anchovies, soaked in water for 15 minutes, drained and chopped

¼ cup chopped basil

4 shallots, minced

2 tablespoons drained capers

2 tablespoons freshly grated Parmesan

⅓ cup chopped walnuts

Freshly ground pepper, to taste

Rub olive oil over peppers and arrange on a baking sheet, cut side up. In a small bowl, combine tomatoes, anchovies, basil, shallots, and capers. Place a teaspoon or more of the mixture on each wedge of pepper. Bake in a preheated 400-degree oven for 20 minutes. Remove from the oven and sprinkle with Parmesan, walnuts, and pepper. Return to the oven and bake 10 minutes more. Place peppers under a broiler for 2 to 3 minutes, or until they char slightly. Serve hot or at room temperature. These peppers can be made in advance and reheated in a microwave.

YIELD: 8 SERVINGS

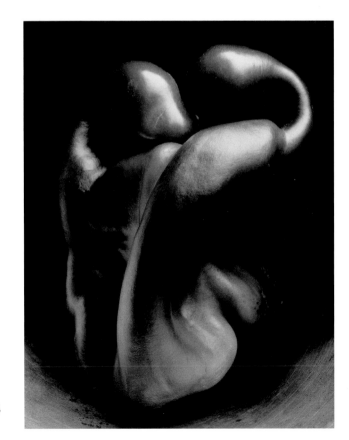

EDWARD WESTON, 1886–1958
Pepper, 1930

Skillet Tomatoes

2 pounds grape or cherry
    tomatoes, divided
2 tablespoons extra virgin
    olive oil
1 tablespoon butter
3 scallions, chopped
1 clove garlic, minced
1 tablespoon chopped rosemary
1 tablespoon chopped parsley
1 tablespoon chopped dill
¼ teaspoon salt

Slice half the tomatoes in two, leaving the others whole to create an attractive appearance. Heat oil and butter in a large skillet, and sauté scallions and garlic until soft. Add tomatoes, herbs, and salt. Cook just until tomatoes soften but hold their shape.

VARIATION: Add asparagus tips at the same time as the tomatoes.

YIELD: 6 TO 8 SERVINGS

Microwave Szechuan Green Beans

6 cloves garlic
2 quarter-size slices ginger,
    peeled
2 scallions, trimmed and cut
    into 2-inch lengths
1 tablespoon vegetable oil
1 teaspoon red pepper flakes,
    crushed
1 tablespoon soy sauce
1 tablespoon rice wine vinegar
1 pound green beans, trimmed
½ cup coarsely grated radish
    (optional)

Place garlic, ginger, and scallions in a food processor and process until finely chopped. Remove to a 14 × 11 × 2-inch glass or other microwaveable dish. Add oil and red pepper flakes. Cook at 100 percent power for 3 minutes. Remove from microwave. Stir in soy sauce, vinegar, and beans. Cook, uncovered, at 100 percent power for 8 to 10 minutes, stirring twice. Stir again, garnish with radish, if desired, and serve hot or at room temperature.

YIELD: 6 SERVINGS

Succotash with a Dash

¼ pound lean, sliced bacon

1 small onion, chopped

2 garlic cloves, minced

2 cups fresh corn kernels

1 large jalapeño pepper, seeded
 and finely chopped

1 (10-ounce) package frozen
 baby lima beans, thawed

½ pound okra, cut into
 ⅓-inch-thick slices

¾ pound cherry tomatoes
 (1 pint), halved

2 tablespoons cider vinegar,
 or to taste

¼ cup chopped basil

Salt, to taste

Pepper, to taste

Cook bacon in a large skillet over moderate heat until crisp. Remove bacon from the pan, drain on paper towels, crumble, and set aside. Pour off excess fat. Add onion to the skillet and sauté until softened. Stir in garlic and sauté 1 minute. Add corn, jalapeño, lima beans, okra, and tomatoes and cook, stirring, until vegetables are tender, 7 to 10 minutes. Stir in vinegar, basil, salt, and pepper. Serve succotash with crumbled bacon on top.

YIELD: 6 TO 8 SERVINGS

The Indian name "m'sickquatash" means the corn grains are whole (not ground into meal). This updated version is tastier than the original recipe the Native Americans offered the first settlers.

Kalyx-krater (mixing bowl) with Dionysos,
a satyr, and a maenad
Greek, South Italian, Late Classical Period,
about 345–335 B.C.

Red Bliss Potato Salad with Vinaigrette

2 pounds small red bliss
   potatoes, scrubbed
1 pint cherry tomatoes, halved
1 tablespoon extra virgin
   olive oil
1 teaspoon coarse salt
1 teaspoon freshly ground
   black pepper
2 hard-cooked eggs
1 cup minced celery

VINAIGRETTE
½ cup red wine vinegar
½ cup finely chopped cooked
   bacon
½ cup finely chopped shallots
1 tablespoon honey
2 teaspoons salt
1 teaspoon freshly ground black
   pepper
⅔ cup extra virgin olive oil

Place potatoes in a saucepan and add water to cover. Bring to a boil, reduce heat to medium, and cook until just tender, about 15 minutes. Drain, rinse with cold water, and refrigerate. Toss tomatoes with oil, salt, and pepper and roast in a preheated 400-degree oven for 3 minutes; refrigerate until needed. Put all vinaigrette ingredients except oil into a blender; blend at medium speed, adding the oil slowly. Slice potatoes and eggs ¼ inch thick, and place in a large mixing bowl. Add tomatoes, celery, and vinaigrette; gently fold mixture until ingredients are combined.

YIELD: 5 SERVINGS (7 CUPS)

Maple Smashed Sweet Potatoes

4 large sweet potatoes
1 tablespoon unsalted butter,
   softened
2 tablespoons sour cream
2 tablespoons pure maple syrup
Salt, to taste
Freshly ground black pepper,
   to taste

Scrub potatoes and pierce them with a fork. Bake in a preheated 375-degree oven for 45 to 50 minutes, until soft; let cool slightly. When potatoes are cool enough to handle, cut them in half lengthwise and scoop the pulp into a bowl, discarding skins. Add butter, sour cream, and maple syrup. With a fork or potato masher, blend the ingredients, leaving lots of potato chunks. Season to taste with salt and pepper.

YIELD: 4 SERVINGS

These potatoes can be made ahead and reheated in a 350-degree oven for 30 minutes.

Sweet Potato Pie

3 tablespoons flour

1⅔ cups sugar

1 cup peeled, cooked, mashed sweet potatoes (2 to 3 potatoes)

2 eggs

¼ cup light corn syrup

¼ teaspoon ground cardamom

⅛ teaspoon salt

½ cup butter, softened

¾ cup evaporated milk

1 (9-inch) unbaked pastry shell

In a large mixing bowl, combine flour and sugar. Add potatoes, eggs, corn syrup, cardamom, salt, butter, and evaporated milk. Beat well. Pour into pastry shell. Bake in a preheated 350-degree oven for 55 to 60 minutes.

YIELD: 8 SERVINGS

To make ahead, bake the pie for only 45 minutes and finish baking the next day. This vegetable pie is perfect for Thanksgiving, when its sweetness balances the tartness of cranberry sauce. It is a pleasant dessert any time of year; just garnish with whipped cream.

Picnics

Whatever the season, you'll enjoy your outdoor adventures even more when you can elevate everyone's spirits with surprises from your picnic basket:

- London Mimosa (page 35) or Passion Fruit Punch (page 35)
- Marinated Shrimp (page 27) or Marinated Mushrooms (page 22)
- Grilled Vegetable Gazpacho (page 44)
- Red Bliss Potato Salad with Vinaigrette (page 141)
- Solar Summer Salad (page 63)
- Black Bean Salad (page 58)
- Mediterranean Stuffed Chicken Breasts (page 95)
- Pinwheel Meatloaf (page 112)
- Sun-dried Tomato Herb Bread (page 75)
- Norwegian Spiced Cookies (page 169)

Potato Puff

5 pounds potatoes, peeled
 and cut into pieces
1 cup sour cream
1 (8-ounce) package cream
 cheese, softened
⅛ teaspoon garlic powder
1 teaspoon salt
¼ teaspoon pepper
2 tablespoons butter, softened
Paprika

In a large pot, cook potatoes in boiling water until tender. Drain and mash until smooth. Add sour cream, cream cheese, garlic powder, salt, and pepper. Beat until light and fluffy. Put the potatoes in a greased 2-quart baking dish, dot with butter, and bake in a preheated 350-degree oven for 30 minutes. Sprinkle with paprika before serving.

YIELD: 8 TO 10 SERVINGS

This puff can be prepared in advance and refrigerated before baking. If it has been refrigerated, bake for 45 minutes.

Potato Pancakes with Scallions and Prosciutto

6 medium red potatoes
¾ cup minced scallions
¼ pound prosciutto, minced
2 eggs, lightly beaten
6 tablespoons flour, or more
 if needed
Salt, to taste
½ teaspoon freshly ground
 pepper
¼ to ½ cup vegetable oil

Line one baking sheet with paper towels and another with aluminum foil. Peel potatoes and grate or shred into a bowl. Add scallions, prosciutto, eggs, flour, salt, and pepper. Mix to blend, adding a little more flour if the mixture is too liquid. Heat 2 to 3 tablespoons oil in a large heavy skillet. When oil is hot but not smoking, drop full tablespoons of the potato mixture into the hot oil, flattening each mound with a spatula. Fry for about 1 minute on each side, or until pancakes are golden brown and crisp. Remove with a slotted spatula, drain on the paper-towel-lined baking sheet, and arrange in one layer on the foil-lined sheet. Change the towels as they absorb oil. Place cooked pancakes in a preheated 200-degree oven to keep warm. Continue frying, adding more oil as necessary.

YIELD: 1 DOZEN 3-INCH PANCAKES

Grains

Fresh Bread Crumbs

Crumble fresh bread slices. If using an unsliced loaf, cut off the ends and pull out small crumbs with a fork. Use crusts or not, as you like. To make Buttered Fresh Bread Crumbs, melt 2 tablespoons butter in a skillet over medium-high heat. Add the crumbs from 3 slices of bread, toss, and sauté for about 3 minutes, or until crumbs are golden.

YIELD: ABOUT ¾ CUP

Cornbread Stuffing

½ cup butter

1 small onion, chopped

2 ribs celery, chopped

3 Golden Delicious apples, peeled, cored, and diced

½ cup unsalted cashew halves

4½ cups bite-size pieces corn muffin

4¾ cups bite-size cubes day-old bread (any combination of sweet or herb breads)

½ cup golden raisins (optional)

1 cup chicken stock, to moisten as desired

Salt, to taste

Pepper, to taste

Melt butter in a large skillet, and sauté onion and celery just until soft. Add apples and cashews, cook a few more minutes, and set aside. In a large bowl, mix muffin pieces and bread cubes. Add apple mixture and raisins and toss until evenly distributed. Gradually add chicken stock to stuffing mixture, stirring it in a little at a time until the desired firmness is reached. Bake in a greased 13 × 9 × 2-inch baking pan in a preheated 350-degree oven for 30 to 40 minutes, or until the top is crusty and golden. The middle will be moist, not soggy.

YIELD: 9 CUPS

This stuffing is rich and satisfying. The recipe may be doubled.

Baked Semolina Gnocchi

½ cup unsalted butter, divided

2 to 3 tablespoons chopped
   basil

6 cups milk

1½ cups semolina flour

2 eggs, slightly beaten

1½ teaspoons salt

1 cup freshly grated Parmesan,
   divided

Freshly ground pepper, to taste

In a small skillet over low heat, melt 6 tablespoons butter, add basil, stir to mix, and set aside. In a large saucepan over medium heat, bring milk to a simmer. Slowly add semolina in a steady stream, stirring constantly with a wooden spoon until very thick, about 5 to 6 minutes. Reduce heat to low and beat eggs in quickly to prevent them from coagulating; continue to stir and cook for 2 minutes longer. Turn off the heat; stir in butter mixture, salt, and ¾ cup Parmesan; beat with the wooden spoon until dough is smooth and glossy. Pour dough into a buttered 13 × 9 × 2-inch baking dish, smooth the surface, and refrigerate for several hours, until cool and firm. (Recipe may be made one day ahead up to this point.) Cut dough into 12 squares, and then cut each square diagonally in half to form 24 triangles. Using a spatula, lift the pieces to a large buttered baking dish, allowing space between each triangle. Melt remaining 2 tablespoons butter and drizzle it over the triangles; sprinkle with remaining ¼ cup Parmesan. Bake gnocchi in a preheated 400-degree oven for 20 to 25 minutes, or until golden brown. Season with freshly ground pepper.

YIELD: 24 TRIANGLES   *This easy version of gnocchi may be served as a side dish or a first course.*

Boston Baked Beans

1 pound small white or navy
   beans
½ pound bacon
3 cups chopped onions
2 cloves garlic, minced
2 teaspoons dry mustard
½ teaspoon ground ginger
2 teaspoons salt
½ teaspoon pepper
½ cup dark brown sugar
1 cup molasses
3 to 6 tablespoons cider
   vinegar, to taste for sweet
   or savory
1 cup tomato sauce
3 to 4 cups reserved bean stock
   or water

Wash beans, cover with 4 cups cold water, and soak overnight. Drain beans and rinse with cold water. Place beans in a 3-quart saucepan with cold water to cover and bring to a boil; reduce heat to simmer, partially cover, and cook slowly for 30 minutes or until tender. Drain beans when they are done, reserving the cooking liquid. Sauté bacon over medium heat for 10 minutes, or until golden brown and crisp; remove bacon from the pan, cool, and crumble. Sauté onions and garlic in bacon fat until soft and translucent; add mustard, ginger, salt, pepper, and sugar. In a large 3-quart baking dish or bean pot, combine onion mixture with beans. Blend in bacon, molasses, vinegar, tomato sauce, and bean stock or water. Bake beans, covered, in a preheated 300-degree oven for 3 hours; uncover and bake for ½ to 1 hour, until beans are soft and liquid has thickened to a sauce.

VARIATIONS: For vegetarian beans, sauté onions and garlic in 2 tablespoons vegetable oil instead of bacon fat and add 3 medium tomatoes, chopped, or 3 medium tart apples cut into ½-inch chunks.

YIELD: 6 TO 8 SERVINGS

This classic dish, which gave Boston its nickname "Beantown," boasts rich, dark brown beans flavored with molasses, as in the Colonial version, but updated here for today's taste. Earlier recipes featured only beans, salt pork, molasses, mustard, and water. A traditional favorite for Saturday night supper, baked beans are still a popular side dish for breakfast, lunch, or dinner at several well known old Boston restaurants. Serve with Boston Brown Bread (page 74).

Wild Rice with Mushrooms

1 cup wild rice

1 cup cold water

2 tablespoons minced onion

1 cup sliced mushrooms, domestic or wild

3 tablespoons butter, divided

3 slices bacon, cooked and crumbled

¼ cup or more heavy cream, to moisten

Rinse rice in cold water, place in a saucepan, and cover with fresh cold water. Cook, uncovered, 20 to 30 minutes, until half the kernels have opened. Remove rice from the heat, cover, and let stand. Sauté onion and mushrooms in 2 tablespoons butter; set aside. Melt remaining butter in a large skillet, and sauté rice to set the kernels and preserve the texture. Add onion, mushrooms, bacon, and enough cream to moisten rice lightly. Place in a baking dish and bake, uncovered, in a preheated 350-degree oven for 20 to 25 minutes.

YIELD: 4 TO 6 SERVINGS

Cumin Basmati Rice

½ pound lean bacon, minced

½ cup shallots, minced

5 teaspoons pine nuts (about 1 ounce)

2 cups sliced mushrooms (about ½ pound)

2½ cups basmati rice (about 1 pound)

4 cups chicken stock

1 tablespoon cumin

1 teaspoon white pepper

In a deep, heavy skillet, sauté bacon and shallots at high heat until golden brown. Add pine nuts, mushrooms, and rice, and sauté 4 minutes; stir in chicken stock, cumin, and pepper. Bring mixture to a boil, cover, and turn heat to low. Simmer for 20 minutes.

YIELD: 8 SERVINGS

Fruited Pilaf

½ cup butter

I garlic clove, minced

4 scallions, sliced

2 cups long grain white rice

½ teaspoon ground ginger

I cup dried apricots, diced

4½ cups beef stock

I cup slivered blanched
almonds

½ cup flaked coconut

Melt butter in a 4-quart saucepan; add garlic, scallions, and rice. Sauté until rice is golden, stirring frequently. Stir in ginger, apricots, and stock; heat to boiling. Cover and cook over low heat for 20 to 25 minutes. Meanwhile, spread almonds in a greased baking pan and bake in a preheated 350-degree oven for 5 to 7 minutes or until brown, stirring frequently. In another greased pan, bake coconut for about 5 minutes or until golden, stirring occasionally. Combine almonds with rice and sprinkle with coconut.

YIELD: 8 TO 10 SERVINGS

Condiments

New England Baked Cranberry Sauce

6 cups fresh or frozen
    cranberries
1½ cups packed brown sugar
1 cup plus 2 tablespoons pure
    maple syrup, divided
1 cup bourbon

Wash, pick over, and drain cranberries. In a 2½- to 3-quart ovenproof baking dish, layer cranberries and brown sugar; pour 1 cup syrup and then 1 cup bourbon over cranberries. Baking temperature and time can be adjusted to cook the sauce along with other food in the oven; for example, bake uncovered in a preheated 350-degree oven for 1½ hours or a 200-degree oven for 2½ to 3 hours. Stir the mixture after the first 15 minutes and then occasionally during baking to dissolve the sugar and push the berries down into the liquid. Before the last half-hour of baking, stir once again and then drizzle remaining 2 tablespoons syrup over the top. Serve warm, at room temperature, or cold.

YIELD: 7 CUPS

Cranberry sauce makes a pleasant accompaniment to the meat course, and leftover sauce served with ice cream is a treat that should not be denied, so be sure to prepare enough. The sauce will keep in the refrigerator for 2 to 3 months.

Wild cranberries provided nourishment to Native Americans and settlers alike. Today, the harvesting of cultivated fruit from cranberry bogs is an important industry on Cape Cod. The brilliant red berries are used in cookies, muffins, pies, and puddings, and the juice makes a delicious tart beverage.

JAMES PEALE, 1749–1831
A Porcelain Bowl with Fruit, 1830

Cranberry, Apple, and Pear Chutney

2 cups fresh or frozen
   cranberries
2 cups peeled, cored, chopped
   Granny Smith apples
2 cups peeled, cored, chopped
   green Bartlett pears
½ cup golden raisins
1½ cups brown sugar
1 cup water
½ cup cider vinegar
1 teaspoon freshly grated ginger
1 teaspoon allspice
1 teaspoon cloves

Wash, pick over, and drain cranberries. Place all ingredients in a large saucepan and cook over medium-high heat, stirring, until the mixture comes to a boil. Reduce the heat and simmer, stirring occasionally, until fruit is tender and chutney has the consistency of salsa, about 35 minutes. Cool; refrigerate, covered, for up to 1 week.

YIELD: ABOUT 6 CUPS

Apricot Onion Chutney

½ pound dried apricots,
   quartered
1½ cups golden raisins
2 cups white vinegar
2 large onions, chopped
1 clove garlic, minced
¼ cup slivered almonds
½ cup dark brown sugar
1 teaspoon freshly grated ginger
⅛ teaspoon cayenne
Salt, to taste
Pepper, to taste

Soak apricots and raisins in vinegar overnight. Put onions in a saucepan, cover with water, bring to a boil, and simmer until soft and translucent. Drain onions, reserving water. Mix all ingredients together, and add enough reserved water to cover; boil for 30 minutes, stirring constantly. Serve as a condiment with any meat dish or as an hors d'oeuvre with crackers and cream cheese.

YIELD: 1 QUART

This South African chutney is also known as blatjang.

LEVI WELLS PRENTICE, 1851–1935
Apples in a Tin Pail, 1892

L.W.Prentice. 1892

Red Onion Marmalade

¼ cup extra virgin olive oil
2 large red onions, sliced
⠀⠀¼ inch thick
½ cup red wine
¼ cup red wine vinegar
¼ cup water
2 teaspoons sugar
½ teaspoon salt
¼ teaspoon freshly ground
⠀⠀pepper

Heat oil over low heat in a medium skillet. Sauté onions until very soft, stirring often, about 15 to 20 minutes. Add wine, vinegar, water, and sugar and raise heat to medium. Cook uncovered for about 15 minutes. Season with salt and pepper.

YIELD: 2 CUPS

Accompaniments for Curry

Golden raisins
Unpeeled, cored, diced
⠀⠀tart apples
Sliced bananas
Orange segments
Chutney
Chopped scallions
Chopped parsley

Chopped bell peppers
Chopped cashews
Chopped peanuts
Chopped hard-cooked egg whites
Chopped hard-cooked egg yolks
Crumbled cooked bacon
Unsweetened coconut
Sautéed poppadum (Indian wafers)

Place selected accompaniments in individual bowls; arrange bowls on a tray for guests to serve themselves.

Citrus Butter

1 orange
1 lemon
1 lime
1 teaspoon salt
1 teaspoon white pepper
1 cup unsalted butter, softened

Remove peel and juice from orange, lemon, and lime. Finely mince peel and add to juice. Mix in salt and pepper. Whip butter and gradually blend juice into butter until all liquid is incorporated. Spoon mixture into a sealable container and refrigerate. Use a melon baller to scoop a portion from the container and serve on grilled or baked seafood or with vegetables such as asparagus.

YIELD: 10 SERVINGS

Wasabi Butter

½ cup butter, softened
2 to 3 teaspoons wasabi powder

Whip softened butter with 2 to 3 teaspoons wasabi powder until thoroughly mixed. Fill a small container with the butter and chill until very firm. Wasabi butter curls make a novel garnish for steak or fish.

YIELD: ½ CUP

Miso Sauce

¼ cup white sesame seeds, toasted
¼ cup sweet miso paste (saikyo miso) or regular white miso plus 2 teaspoons sugar
3 tablespoons mirin (sweetened rice wine)
2 tablespoons sugar

Grind toasted sesame seeds into a paste. Add remaining ingredients and mix well until sugar dissolves. Serve on steamed or baked chicken, grilled eggplant, peppers, mushrooms, or tofu.

YIELD: ½ CUP

Pesto Genovese

1½ cups basil leaves
⅓ cup flatleaf parsley
½ cup extra virgin olive oil
½ cup freshly grated Parmesan
½ cup pine nuts
½ teaspoon salt
2 garlic cloves, minced
2 tablespoons butter

Wash basil and parsley, strip leaves from stems, and pack down firmly to measure. Gradually mix all ingredients in a blender or food processor until smooth (mixture will be rather thick). Serve at room temperature over cooked thin spaghetti or linguine, using ¼ to ½ cup pasta cooking liquid to moisten. For an appetizer, put a dollop on mussels and place briefly under the broiler. Serve as a sandwich dressing or as a condiment with grilled fish or meat. Toss with vegetables.

YIELD: ABOUT 1½ CUPS

Pesto may be prepared ahead; refrigerate for up to 1 week or freeze.

Teriyaki Sauce

¼ cup soy sauce
¼ cup mirin (sweetened rice wine)
2 tablespoons sake
1 tablespoon sugar

Combine ingredients and simmer in saucepan until reduced by half. Brush on grilled chicken or fish.

YIELD: ½ CUP

Mustard Sauce

2 tablespoons white sesame seeds, toasted
½ cup mayonnaise
2 teaspoons Dijon mustard
2 teaspoons soy sauce
1 teaspoon sugar

Grind toasted sesame seeds. Add remaining ingredients and mix well. Use as a sauce for steamed or baked chicken or for cooked vegetables, such as cauliflower, broccoli, asparagus, green beans, and brussels sprouts.

YIELD: ½ CUP

YOSHIDA HIROSHI, 1876–1950
Greengrocer, Nezu, Japan, 1926

Fruits,
Custards,
Sweets

The conclusion to your menu deserves
a lovely compote or cake stand. After a grand
meal, your guests may appreciate a simple fruit
dessert. A beautiful pie or chocolate cake, though,
may lure them into believing there is still room
for more. Spread your culinary wings as you
choose from the many elegant possibilities suggested here. The final course, presented with
care and imagination, becomes the perfect
finishing touch.

Chair, 1985
Made by JAY STANGER, born 1956

Fruits

Melon Balls with Lime Sauce

1 cup vanilla yogurt
2 tablespoons lime juice
1 tablespoon grated lime peel
2 teaspoons light brown sugar
½ teaspoon cinnamon
1 large honeydew
1 large cantaloupe
Mint sprigs

Combine yogurt, lime juice and peel, sugar, and cinnamon and let stand for 4 hours or overnight. Use a large melon scoop to make balls, or cut melons into ¾-inch squares. Place sauce in a bowl, surround with melon pieces, and garnish with mint. Serve with cocktail picks.

YIELD: 12 TO 16 SERVINGS

The sauce goes well with many fruits and berries.

Melons in Sweet Wine

½ cantaloupe
¼ honeydew
¼ casaba
1 cup sweet white wine, such
   as Muscadet or Riesling
1 teaspoon minced candied
   ginger

Using a 1-inch scoop, cut melon balls into a bowl; add wine and ginger, mixing well. Cover and refrigerate overnight. To serve, arrange melon balls in dessert dishes and spoon wine sauce over.

YIELD: 4 SERVINGS

Soleggiata Serena, 2000
Made by TOOTS ZYNSKY, born 1951

Oranges Aviz

6 navel oranges or a combination of 3 navel and 3 blood oranges
½ cup cold water
½ cup grenadine
1½ cups sugar
½ pint fresh raspberries

Using a vegetable peeler, remove only the top layer of orange skins, avoiding the white pith. Thinly julienne peel and reserve oranges. In a heavy saucepan, combine water, grenadine, and sugar; heat slowly until sugar has dissolved and then boil until syrup registers 235 degrees on a candy thermometer. Add peels and simmer for 2 minutes. Cool and refrigerate in a covered container until ready to use. Remove pith remaining on oranges. Slice oranges crosswise and arrange in a shallow glass bowl or plate. Add raspberries. Lift orange peels out of syrup with a fork and swirl over the fruit. (To make ahead, follow the directions for preparing peel and use the orange flesh for another purpose; finish the dessert by selecting new oranges and discarding their peel.)

YIELD: 4 TO 6 SERVINGS

This is a Boston version of Portugal's best orange dessert.

Summer Pudding

¼ pound red currants

½ pound black currants

½ pound raspberries

½ to 1 cup sugar, to taste

Butter

Slices of day-old white bread, crusts removed, a loaf or more

Heavy cream, whipped cream, or vanilla ice cream

Rinse and pick over currants and raspberries; combine with sugar in a saucepan. Cook mixture gently for 2½ minutes, or until berries have released their juices; set aside to cool. Line a deep pudding bowl or charlotte mold with plastic wrap, extending the wrap over the rim. Next, line the bowl with slices of white bread trimmed and fitted to eliminate gaps through which juices can escape. Ladle a third of the berry mixture into the bowl and cover with a layer of bread; repeat this step twice, reserving some juice. Cover the final layer of bread with plastic wrap; set a plate on top, and on the plate put sufficient weight to compress the whole bowl of pudding. Refrigerate overnight. To finish, remove the top piece of plastic wrap and invert the pudding onto a serving plate; pour reserved juice over pudding to moisten and decorate. Serve with heavy cream, whipped cream, or vanilla ice cream.

YIELD: 4 SERVINGS

A traditional English pudding, this dessert can be made a day or two ahead. Use any combination of two to three kinds of ripe berries, amounting to 6 cups, sweetened accordingly. A sweet egg bread, like brioche or challah, sliced ⅜ to ½ inch thick can be substituted for white bread.

Fresh Fruit Brûlé

SYRUP

½ cup sugar

⅔ cup water

2 tablespoons Cointreau or
brandy

FRUIT

4 peaches, peeled, pitted,
and thinly sliced

2 firm bananas, peeled
and sliced

4 kiwi, peeled, halved,
and sliced

4 plums, pitted and thinly
sliced

2 cups halved seedless grapes

½ cup blanched slivered or
shaved almonds, toasted

TOPPING

⅔ cup heavy cream

¼ teaspoon vanilla

2 tablespoons confectioners'
sugar

⅔ to 1 cup brown sugar

Heat sugar and water in a saucepan, without stirring, until sugar has dissolved; boil rapidly for about 5 minutes. Remove from heat and let cool; stir in Cointreau. In a 12 × 8 × 2-inch heatproof serving dish, layer peaches, bananas, kiwi, plums, grapes, and almonds. Pour syrup over layered ingredients. Whip cream, vanilla, and confectioners' sugar until thick; spoon over the fruit mixture. Sprinkle brown sugar evenly on top and put under a preheated broiler for 2 to 3 minutes, until the sugar has caramelized. Remove from the broiler, let cool, cover with foil, and refrigerate until serving time.

YIELD: 8 TO 10 SERVINGS

The fresh fruit for this dessert can vary with the season. Try strawberries, raspberries, blueberries, and ripe pears. The recipe doubles easily and can be made ahead.

Custards

Lighter Custard Sauce

1½ cups milk, 1 percent or
  skim
2 eggs, or ½ cup egg substitute
⅓ cup sugar
2 teaspoons vanilla
Fruit or cake

Rinse a heavy saucepan with cold water and shake it dry to help prevent sticking. Add milk and bring to a simmer. In a small bowl, whisk eggs with sugar until mixture is smooth but not frothy. Gradually add ¼ cup hot milk to egg mixture and then return warmed egg mixture to the simmering milk. Cook custard over low heat, stirring constantly until the mixture thickens enough to coat the back of a wooden spoon, about 7 to 8 minutes. Do not boil. As custard thickens, continue stirring to prevent curdling. If necessary, strain custard into a clean bowl. Add vanilla and mix well. Cover and chill sauce before serving; it will thicken further as it cools. Serve with fruit or a plain cake.

YIELD: 2¾ CUPS

Peach Velvet

4 very ripe peaches, peeled
   and pitted
1½ cups sugar
2 tablespoons lemon juice
½ teaspoon vanilla
2 egg whites, stiffly beaten
1 cup heavy cream, whipped
2 teaspoons orange curaçao
   (optional)
Sliced peaches
Sliced almonds

In a food processor, purée peaches, sugar, lemon juice, and vanilla until sugar has dissolved; transfer mixture to a large bowl. Fold stiffly beaten egg whites and then whipped cream into peach mixture. Add curaçao, if desired. Chill. Layer with peach slices in individual sherbet dishes and top with sliced almonds.

YIELD: 8 TO 10 SERVINGS

Celestial Crème

1 envelope plain gelatin
   (2¼ teaspoons)
¼ cup cold water
2 cups heavy cream
1 cup superfine sugar
2 cups sour cream
1 teaspoon vanilla
Fresh raspberries, strawberries,
   or blueberries

Sprinkle gelatin into water to dissolve; let stand 2 minutes. Combine cream and sugar in a 1-quart saucepan, add gelatin, and cook over low heat (do not boil), stirring gently, until sugar and gelatin are dissolved. Remove from the heat and let cool. In a large bowl, stir sour cream and vanilla together. Slowly fold cooked mixture into sour cream and then pour it all into a lightly oiled 4-cup ring mold or a glass serving bowl. Chill overnight. Unmold onto a chilled platter or spoon from the serving bowl onto dessert plates, and garnish with berries.

YIELD: 8 TO 10 SERVINGS

Make this dessert a day ahead to give it time to set. For a low-fat alternative, substitute evaporated skim milk for cream and use fat-free sour cream.

UNIDENTIFIED ARTIST,
mid-19th century
Egg Salad, about 1850

Cream Kadayif

FILLING

⅜ cup cornstarch

3 tablespoons sugar

I cup milk, divided

2 cups heavy cream

I½ teaspoons vanilla

Peel of ½ lemon, minced
(optional)

SYRUP

2 cups sugar

I½ cups water

Juice of ½ lemon

PASTRY

I pound shredded phyllo dough
(kadayif)

¾ pound butter, melted

Mix cornstarch and sugar with ⅓ cup milk and set aside. Heat remaining milk and cream in a saucepan over medium heat. Add cornstarch mixture to the warm liquid and cook until thickened, stirring frequently. Remove from heat; stir in vanilla and, if desired, lemon peel. Cover with plastic wrap and refrigerate until ready to use. In another saucepan, bring sugar, water, and lemon juice to a boil and let simmer for ½ hour. Remove the saucepan from the burner and set aside so that syrup will cool to room temperature. Separate the shreds of dough, placing them in a large bowl. When all the strands have been separated, add melted butter, a third at a time, working it completely into the dough. Spread half the dough on the bottom of a 13 × 9 × 2-inch baking pan. Spread cream filling evenly and cover with remaining dough. Bake in a preheated 400-degree oven for 30 minutes, or until top is golden. Remove from the oven and immediately pour cooled syrup over hot kadayif. Cover tightly with foil and let rest for at least ½ hour before cutting and serving.

YIELD: 15 SERVINGS

Shredded phyllo dough is available at Middle Eastern stores. This dessert surprises guests because kadayif, when baked, looks like shredded coconut.

Baked Indian Pudding

4 cups milk, divided
½ cup molasses
1 teaspoon salt
½ cup yellow cornmeal
¼ cup brown sugar
1 teaspoon cinnamon
¾ teaspoon ground ginger
1 tablespoon butter
1 egg, beaten
Vanilla ice cream or whipped
　　cream

Mix 2 cups milk and molasses in the top of a double boiler. Combine salt, cornmeal, sugar, and spices, and add to milk-molasses mixture. Add butter and cook 20 minutes over simmering water, stirring occasionally. Mix egg with 1 cup milk and add. Stir, then pour into a greased 1½-quart baking dish, and bake in a preheated 325-degree oven for 1 hour. Pour 1 cup cold milk over top of pudding. Do not stir. Bake 1 hour longer. Serve warm with a scoop of vanilla ice cream or whipped cream.

YIELD: 6 SERVINGS

In 1621 William Bradford, governor of Plymouth Colony, proclaimed the first Thanksgiving. His wife, a remarkable cook, was known for her Indian pudding, a recipe given her by the Wampanoag Indians.

Maple Syrup Pudding Cake

SYRUP
2 tablespoons cornstarch
1½ cups maple or brown sugar
1 cup pure maple syrup
1½ cups water
1½ tablespoons butter

BATTER
½ cup butter, softened
1 cup sugar
2 eggs
1½ cups flour
2½ tablespoons baking powder
⅛ teaspoon salt
¾ cup milk

In a medium saucepan, combine cornstarch and sugar and mix with maple syrup. Add water slowly and bring to a boil, stirring, over medium-high heat; remove from the heat and add butter. For the batter, cream butter and sugar in a large bowl; add eggs, one at a time, mixing well after each addition. Sift together flour, baking powder, and salt; then alternate adding flour and milk to egg mixture, beating until smooth. Pour syrup into a greased 13 × 9 × 2-inch baking pan. Using a large serving spoon, float batter on syrup to make a cover. Bake in a preheated 375-degree oven for about 40 minutes, or until golden brown and cake has shrunk slightly away from the sides of the pan. Serve hot or at room temperature.

YIELD: 8 SERVINGS

Sweets

Apple Peach Crumble

1½ cups sugar

3 tablespoons cornstarch

6 to 8 Granny Smith apples,
   peeled, cored, and cut into
   ½-inch slices

6 to 8 ripe peaches, peeled,
   pitted, and cut into ½-inch
   slices

1 tablespoon lemon juice

2 teaspoons grated lemon peel

1¼ teaspoons almond extract

Ice cream

TOPPING

1 cup flour

1 cup light brown sugar

⅔ cup old-fashioned oatmeal

1 teaspoon cinnamon

½ cup cold butter, cut into
   pieces

⅔ cup slivered almonds

In a large bowl, combine sugar and cornstarch; mix in apples, peaches, juice, peel, and extract. Pour into a greased 13 × 9 × 2-inch baking dish. Bake in a preheated 400-degree oven for approximately 60 minutes, until juices begin to bubble. For the topping, combine flour, brown sugar, oatmeal, and cinnamon in a medium bowl. Add butter and mix until texture is like coarse meal; stir in almonds. Sprinkle topping over fruit and bake for another 25 minutes or until topping is brown. Serve warm with ice cream.

YIELD: 12 SERVINGS

For convenience, make a large amount of topping and store it in the freezer to be used as needed.

LU ZONGGUI, 13th century
*Orange, Grapes and Pomegranates Square
Album Leaf*

Apple Cheese Torte

CRUST

½ cup butter, softened

⅓ cup sugar

¼ teaspoon vanilla

¾ cup flour

½ cup finely ground walnuts

FILLING

8 ounces cream cheese,
    softened

¼ cup sugar

1 egg

½ teaspoon vanilla

2 medium-sized apples,
    peeled, cored, and thinly
    sliced

2 teaspoons sugar

¼ teaspoon cinnamon

Cream together butter, sugar, and vanilla until well blended. Stir in flour and walnuts and mix well. Press the mixture into an ungreased 9-inch springform pan, pressing it 1 inch up the side of the pan. Set aside.

In a medium bowl, beat together cream cheese, sugar, egg, and vanilla until mixture is smooth and creamy; pour over the crust. Starting in the center, arrange apple slices in two rows to form a circular pattern on the cream cheese mixture. Combine sugar and cinnamon; sprinkle over apples. Bake torte in a preheated 350-degree oven for 50 minutes. Cool on a rack for 20 to 30 minutes at room temperature; refrigerate until serving time.

YIELD: 8 SERVINGS

Fresh Blueberry Tart

4 cups blueberries, divided
1 cup sugar
¾ cup plus 3 to 4 tablespoons
    water, divided
1 tablespoon cornstarch
2 tablespoons flour
Squeeze of lemon juice
1 (9-inch) pastry shell, baked
Ice cream

Bring to a boil 1 cup berries, sugar, and ¾ cup water. Mix cornstarch and flour with remaining cold water; whisk until smooth and add to berries. Simmer for 5 minutes. Remove from heat and add 3 cups uncooked berries and lemon juice. Cool slightly, pour into pastry shell, and allow filling to set. Serve with ice cream.

YIELD: 6 TO 8 SERVINGS

Peach Pie Surprise

1 (9-inch) pie shell, unbaked
3 peaches
2 tablespoons butter, softened
1 cup sugar
2 eggs

Place pie shell in a 9-inch glass pie pan. To peel peaches easily, drop them in boiling water for 1 minute and remove skins with a knife. Cut 2 peaches in half, remove pits, and place cut side down in pie shell. Cut remaining peach into slices and scatter around the 4 halves. Bake in a preheated 400-degree oven for 25 minutes. Remove from the oven and lower temperature to 350 degrees. Mix butter and sugar together, add eggs, and beat until very thick, about 5 minutes. Pour over peaches. Return pie to oven and bake for another 25 to 30 minutes.

YIELD: 6 TO 8 SERVINGS

Cherry Clafouti

2 cups canned pitted dark,
　　sweet cherries, drained
3 eggs
⅔ cup sugar
⅛ teaspoon salt
⅓ cup flour
¼ cup butter, melted
1 cup cream or whole milk
1 tablespoon vanilla
Confectioners' sugar

Butter a 10-inch pie pan or ceramic baking dish. Arrange cherries in one layer in the prepared dish; set aside. Beat eggs until foamy. Add sugar and salt and beat until mixture is quite thick. Add flour and blend until smooth; mix in butter, milk, and vanilla. Pour batter over cherries. Bake in a preheated 325-degree oven for 45 to 50 minutes, or until top has puffed and browned, and a knife inserted in center comes out clean. Serve warm or at room temperature. Sift generously with confectioners' sugar and cut into wedges.

YIELD: 8 SERVINGS

Clafouti, a French pastry that resembles a custard fruit flan, can easily be made at the last minute with any choice of fruit—pears, plums, apricots, peaches, or apples. The fruit may be canned, frozen, or fresh, sliced ½ inch thick. The traditional preparation uses dark sweet cherries with pits.

Norwegian Spiced Cookies

1 cup butter, softened
1½ cups sugar
1 egg, beaten
1 tablespoon molasses
1¾ cups flour
1¼ teaspoons baking soda
½ teaspoon salt
2 teaspoons cinnamon
2 teaspoons cloves
2 teaspoons ground ginger
Sugar

Cream together butter and sugar; add egg and molasses and mix well. Sift together flour, soda, salt, cinnamon, cloves, and ginger and combine with butter mixture. Form small balls, no larger than 1 inch, and roll them in sugar. Place balls on a baking sheet lined with parchment paper, leaving 2 inches between to allow for spreading. Bake in a preheated 350-degree oven for 8 to 10 minutes.

YIELD: 6 TO 7 DOZEN

Swiss Meringue Tart

3 egg whites, room temperature
½ teaspoon baking powder
¼ teaspoon salt
1 teaspoon vanilla
1 teaspoon water
1 teaspoon white vinegar
1 cup sugar, sifted

Separate eggs while they are cold; place whites in a large mixing bowl and set aside until they reach room temperature, about 30 minutes. Lightly grease an ovenproof serving platter (14 × 10-inch oval), or place a piece of parchment paper on a baking sheet to prepare a free-form tart. Add baking powder, salt, vanilla, water, and vinegar to egg whites; beat with an electric mixer at high speed to combine the ingredients. When the mixture forms soft peaks, gradually add sugar, 1 tablespoon at a time. Beat until the meringue holds very stiff peaks; do not go beyond the glossy stage. Shape meringue on the platter or parchment paper, building up the sides to form a 1-inch rim. Bake in a preheated 250-degree oven for 1 to 1½ hours, until firm and dry, but do not let it brown. Turn off the oven and leave meringue in the oven to cool; this step prevents shrinkage and ensures dryness. At this point, the meringue is ready to fill and serve. Prepare any filling or garnish ahead of time and quickly assemble just before serving.

FILLINGS

- Fresh fruit (strawberries, blueberries, raspberries, kiwis, bananas) garnished with Crème Fraîche (page 68) or whipped cream, sweetened or flavored
- Cold custard, flavored puddings, or mousses topped with sweetened whipped cream
- Ice creams, sorbets, or other frozen combinations spooned in and returned to the freezer for 2 to 3 days
- Lemon curd lightened by folding 1 cup heavy cream, whipped, into curd (a recipe for Lemon Curd can be found in *Boston Tea Parties: Recipes from the Museum of Fine Arts, Boston*)

Garnish the tart according to choice of filling, using roasted nuts, fresh fruits, lemon sauce, rum sauce, chocolate sauce, or whipped cream.

YIELD: 8 SERVINGS

Originally called Pinch Tart, this dessert was first created in a pastry shop in Switzerland in the early 1700s. Today it is enjoyed around the world in many variations and forms. This gala dessert is easy to make and never fails to delight guests!

Hazelnut Cheesecake

1 cup hazelnuts
4 (8-ounce) packages cream
    cheese, softened
1¾ cups sugar
4 eggs
½ teaspoon grated lemon peel
⅓ cup zwieback or graham
    cracker crumbs
Additional hazelnuts

Place hazelnuts on a baking sheet and roast in a pre-heated 350-degree oven until light brown, about 12 minutes. Let cool slightly; rub warm nuts in a dish towel to remove most of the skins. Chop nuts in a blender to an uneven coarseness and set aside. Beat cream cheese in a large bowl until very smooth, scraping the sides of the bowl frequently. Beat sugar in very well, add eggs one at a time, and continue beating only to blend the ingredients. Fold in lemon peel and hazelnuts with a spatula. Pour batter into a greased 8 × 3-inch spring-form pan and spread to level the top. Place cake pan in a larger pan and fill the larger pan with hot water to a depth of 1½ inches. Bake cake in a preheated 350-degree oven for 1 hour and 20 minutes, or until top is golden brown. (If cake appears to be browning too quickly, place a piece of well buttered foil over it.) Set the pan on a rack for 3 hours, or until cheesecake is completely cool. Do not cool in the refrigerator. When the bottom of the pan has reached room temperature, remove the side and invert the cake onto a flat dish. Sprinkle the cake evenly with crumbs. Invert cake again, carefully and quickly, onto a serving plate, so that it is right side up. Decorate with hazelnuts. Refrigerate at least 5 to 6 hours or overnight. To cut, dip knife into hot water between slices to prevent sticking.

YIELD: 8 SERVINGS   *The cake freezes well.*

Fallen Chocolate Soufflé Cake

1 pound bittersweet chocolate,
    coarsely chopped
1 cup unsalted butter
9 eggs, separated
¾ cup sugar, divided
Unsweetened cocoa, for
    dusting
Confectioners' sugar, for
    dusting

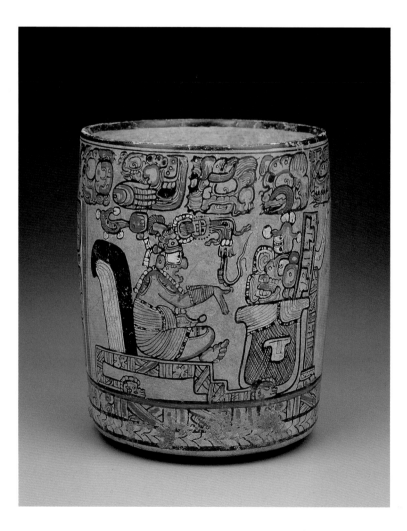

Line the bottom of a 9 × 3-inch springform pan with parchment paper. Lightly butter and flour the paper. Melt chocolate and butter in a double boiler or metal bowl set over barely simmering water. Stir to combine, remove from the heat, and set aside to cool. In a separate bowl, combine egg yolks with all but 1 teaspoon of sugar and beat at high speed until the mixture is light and forms a ribbon when the beaters are lifted from the bowl. In another bowl, combine egg whites with reserved sugar. Beat until the egg whites form soft peaks. Fold one-third of the chocolate mixture into a bowl with one-third of the yolk mixture. Fold in one-third of the egg whites. Repeat two more times, so that all of the ingredients are incorporated. Pour batter into the pan, and bake in a preheated 300-degree oven for 30 minutes. Do not overbake; the center of the cake should still be soft. Let cool to room temperature for 3 hours; do not remove from the pan sooner, or the cake will fall apart. Remove the sides of the springform pan and dust cake with cocoa, then confectioners' sugar, and then cocoa and sugar again. Cover and refrigerate overnight. Before serving, let the cake warm to room temperature. Dust again with cocoa and confectioners' sugar. This cake freezes beautifully undecorated.

DECORATIONS

- Chocolate-dipped strawberries (directions are given in *Boston Tea Parties: Recipes from the Museum of Fine Arts, Boston*).
- Large chocolate curls arranged in modern, vertical, angled forms on top and dusted with confectioners' sugar. To form curls, brush melted chocolate on squares of waxed paper, insert in narrow glasses, and refrigerate.
- Small chocolate curls piled high and dusted with confectioners' sugar. Use a cheese slicer to shave curls from a block of chocolate.
- Chocolate lemon leaves overlapping on top and dusted with confectioners' sugar. Wash and dry large lemon leaves, place on waxed paper vein side up, brush with melted chocolate, and refrigerate.

YIELD: 8 TO 10 SERVINGS

For best results, use fine-quality bittersweet or extra-bittersweet chocolate. In a pinch, use semisweet chocolate and reduce the sugar to ½ cup.

Cylinder vase
Maya, Mexico (Campeche), A.D. 600–750

Chocolate Supreme Mousse Cake Roll

6 ounces dark sweet chocolate

3 tablespoons water

5 eggs, separated

¾ cup sugar

2 tablespoons sugar

I tablespoon cocoa

FILLING

6 ounces dark sweet chocolate,
    coarsely chopped

2 tablespoons sugar

2 tablespoons water

3 eggs, separated

I teaspoon vanilla

¾ cup heavy cream, whipped

Line the bottom of a greased 15 × 10 × 1-inch jellyroll pan with a sheet of foil that extends about 4 inches beyond each of the narrow ends. Grease the foil and fold up the extended edges to form two handles. Melt chocolate with water in the top of a double boiler, stirring until smooth; set aside and cool mixture slightly. Beat egg yolks, gradually add sugar, and continue beating until creamy and pale yellow. Add chocolate and continue beating until well blended. In a separate bowl, beat egg whites until stiff but not dry; gently fold whites into cake batter. Spread the batter evenly in the pan, making sure all corners are filled. Bake in a preheated 350-degree oven for 12 to 15 minutes. Remove from the oven and invert the pan onto a clean towel that has been dusted with a combination of sugar and cocoa. Immediately peel off the foil, trim any crusty edges with a sharp knife, and, starting at a narrow end, roll up the towel and warm cake together. Place on a rack to cool. When cake is ready to fill, unroll it and spread on all but 1 cup of filling. Roll cake again, placing the seam edge down on the serving plate. Refrigerate for at least 4 hours or overnight. Using a sharp, clean knife, slice the cake roll crosswise.

For the filling, melt chocolate and sugar in water in the top of the double boiler; stir constantly until smooth, remove from the heat, and set aside to cool. Beat egg whites until stiff but not dry; set aside. In a separate bowl, beat egg yolks until thick and lemon yellow; add chocolate mixture and vanilla; blend well. Gently fold in beaten egg whites. Fold in whipped cream until blended. Refrigerate for at least 1 hour or until the filling is firm. Reserve 1 cup of filling for decoration. Before serving, use a decorating bag to form rosettes on top or around the edges of the cake roll.

YIELD: 10 TO 12 SERVINGS

The cake roll can be made a day ahead. The filling itself may be served as a mousse, garnished with whipped cream and shaved chocolate.

Grand piano, 1796
Manufactured by John Broadwood
& Son

Pound Cake

1½ cups unsalted butter, softened
4 cups (16-ounce box) sifted confectioners' sugar
6 eggs, room temperature
1 teaspoon vanilla
2¾ cups sifted cake flour
Confectioners' sugar

Beat butter until fluffy. Gradually add confectioners' sugar, beating until thoroughly incorporated. Add eggs, one at a time, beating well after each addition. Stir in vanilla. Add flour gradually, beating until light and fluffy. Pour into a greased and floured 10-inch tube or bundt pan and bake in a preheated 300-degree oven for 1½ hours, or until a tester inserted in the middle comes out clean. Let the cake rest in the pan for 10 minutes. To remove, slide a thin knife around the cake to separate it from the pan before turning it onto a serving platter (if serving soon) or wire rack (if serving at room temperature). Decorate with confectioners' sugar sifted sparingly over the top of the cake.

VARIATION: Cut pound cake into ½-inch slices and arrange on individual dessert plates. Spread each slice with 3 tablespoons sour cream, sprinkle with 1 to 2 tablespoons brown sugar, and top with 3 to 4 peach slices (fresh, frozen, or canned). Garnish with chopped nuts.

YIELD: 8 TO 10 SERVINGS

This very rich cake is somewhat sweeter than the usual pound cake. Berries of any kind make a nice garnish and contrast.

More Cakes and Cookies

Boston Tea Parties: Recipes from the Museum of Fine Arts, Boston offers a large selection of New England's favorite recipes for cookies and bars as well as cakes and other desserts. Boston itself is the birthplace of the chocolate chip cookie, first served at the Toll House Restaurant just south of the city.

Big Dig Mud

Cocoa

2 cups flour

1 teaspoon baking soda

⅛ teaspoon salt

5 (1-ounce) squares
   unsweetened chocolate

1 cup butter, cut into pieces

1¾ cups strong coffee

¼ cup bourbon

2 cups sugar

2 eggs, slightly beaten

1 teaspoon vanilla

Whipped cream

Butter a bundt pan and dust it with cocoa. Sift together flour, baking soda, and salt. In a double boiler over simmering water, melt chocolate and butter; then add coffee and bourbon and mix together until smooth. Add sugar and stir to incorporate. Cool for 3 minutes. Pour mixture into a large bowl. Add flour mixture, ½ cup at a time, and beat at medium speed for 1 minute. Add eggs and vanilla, and beat until smooth. Pour the batter into a pan and bake in a preheated 275-degree oven for 1½ hours, or until a tester inserted in the middle comes out clean. Cool completely in the pan. Serve with whipped cream.

YIELD: 10 TO 12 SERVINGS

This dessert is named in honor of Boston's Central Artery/Tunnel Project, the largest and most tech-nologically challenging highway project ever attempted in American history. Its motto is "The Big Dig—worth the wait." This dessert is worth the weight!

Stela of Ahmose
Egypt, New Kingdom, Dynasty 18, 1539–1292 B.C.

Boston Cream Pie

CREAM CUSTARD
I egg
½ cup sugar
¼ cup flour
⅛ teaspoon salt
I cup milk, divided
½ teaspoon vanilla

SPONGE CAKE
3 eggs, separated
¼ teaspoon cream of tartar
¼ cup cold water
¾ cup sugar
¼ teaspoon salt
½ teaspoon lemon extract
½ teaspoon vanilla
¾ cup sifted cake flour

CHOCOLATE GLAZE
¼ cup cream
⅔ cup chocolate chips

Evening ensemble, winter collection 1935–36
Designed by Jeanne Lavin, 1867–1946

For the custard, in a small bowl, stir egg lightly to combine yolk and white; blend in sugar, flour, and salt; slowly add ½ cup milk and set aside. In a heavy 1-quart saucepan, heat remaining milk and vanilla until scalded; then remove from the heat. Stir a small amount of milk into the egg mixture and then quickly whisk the egg mixture into the hot milk. Return the saucepan to medium-high heat and cook, stirring constantly, until mixture begins to thicken and boils, about 3 to 4 minutes. Reduce heat to low and cook, stirring, for 2 minutes to make sure the mixture will set up. Pour custard into a small bowl, press plastic wrap onto its surface, and chill at least 2 hours. The custard can be made a day ahead.

To make the cake, beat egg whites until foamy, add cream of tartar, and beat until moist, glossy peaks form; set aside. Beat egg yolks until thick and lemon yellow; slowly add water and continue beating until very thick, about 2 to 3 minutes. Slowly add sugar; blend in salt, lemon extract, and vanilla. Fold flour into egg yolk mixture a little at a time. Gently fold egg whites into egg yolk mixture. Pour batter into 2 greased (do not grease the sides) 8-inch round cake pans lined on the bottom with waxed paper, greased, and floured. Bake in a preheated 325-degree oven for 20 to 23 minutes. A cake is done if it springs back when pressed lightly with a finger. Invert onto cake racks. Cool completely before removing from pans. Loosen side of cakes with spatula to release from the pans. Spread cream custard onto the bottom layer to within ½ inch from the edges, cover with top layer, and refrigerate.

For the chocolate glaze, place cream in a small, heavy saucepan over moderate heat until scalded. Add chocolate, stir until partly melted, remove pan from the heat, and continue to stir until chocolate has melted completely. Let stand for 10 to 15 minutes, stirring occasionally. Pour glaze onto the top of the cake and smooth it just to the edge. Chill for 2 hours.

YIELD: 6 TO 8 SERVINGS

A famous American dessert called "pudding-cake pie" was renamed Boston Cream Pie by the Parker House Hotel. When the hotel opened in 1855, it added a chocolate glaze to what has remained one of America's most beloved desserts.

Glacier Bench, 1997
Made by John Lewis, born 1942

List of Works of Art

FRONT COVER: STUART DAVIS
American, 1892–1964
Apples and Jug, 1923
Oil on composition board; 21⅜ × 17¾ in.
Gift of the William H. Lane Foundation, 1990.390

BACK COVER: THOMAS ROWLANDSON
English, 1756–1827
A Footman Spilling the Soup (Directions to Footmen)
Pen, ink, and watercolor on paper; 11¾ × 8⁹⁄₁₆ in.
Gift of John T. Spaulding, 48.88

FRONT COVER FLAP: GUJARI RAGINI
From an illustrated *Ragamala* manuscript
Northern India (Rajasthan, Mewar), about 1730
Opaque watercolor on paper; 14⅞ × 9¾ in.
Ross-Coomaraswamy Collection, 30.643

BACK COVER FLAP: NICHOLAS LANCRET
French, 1690–1745
Luncheon Party in a Park (Déjeuner de jambon), about 1735
Oil on canvas; 21⁵⁄₁₆ × 18⅛ in.
Forsyth Wickes Collection, 65.2649

PAGE 1: Sideboard
Pennsylvania (Philadelphia), 1850–60
Made by Ignatius Lutz, American, 1817–1860
Oak, yellow poplar, marble; 94 × 74 × 25 in.
Gift of the Estate of Richard Bruce E. Lacont, 1990.1

PAGES 2–3: *Cow*
United States, about 1926
Alexander Calder, American, 1898–1976
Brass wire; 18 × 24 in.
Decorative Arts Special Fund, 60.240a–b

PAGE 6: Bench
Massachusetts (Cambridge), 1979
Made by Judy Kensley McKie, American, born 1944
Mahogany, leather; 26¾ × 61¼ × 26⅞ in.
Purchased through funds provided by the National
Endowment for the Arts and the Deborah M. Noonan
Foundation, 1979.284
© Judy Kensley McKie

PAGE 9: Bench
Massachusetts (Jamaica Plain), 1986
Made by Dale Broholm, American, born 1956
Cherry, cherry veneer, plywood, leather;
36½ × 23 × 16¾ in.
Gift of Alan Dinsfriend, 1986.676
© Dale Broholm

PAGE 10: GUSTAVE CAILLEBOTTE
French, 1848–1894
Fruit Displayed on a Stand, about 1881–82
Oil on canvas; 30⅛ × 39⅝ in.
Fanny P. Mason Fund in memory of Alice Thevin,
1979.196

PAGE 14: JEAN FRANCOIS MILLET
French, 1814–1875
Young Woman Churning Butter, about 1848–51
Oil on panel; 22⅜ × 14⅛ in.
Gift of Mrs. John S. Ames, 66.1052

PAGE 19: Bench
Tennessee (Smithville), 1982
Made by Thomas Hucker, American, born 1955
Beefwood, bronze; 16¼ × 91½ × 18½ in.
Purchased through funds provided by the National
Endowment for the Arts, Ethan Allen, Inc., and
the Robert Lehman Foundation, 1982.417
© Thomas Hucker

PAGE 20: UNIDENTIFIED ARTIST
Persian, Timurid painting, 1425–50, mounted in
an album, 1544–45
Prince and Lady under Flowering Branch, page from an album
made for Prince Bahrain Mirza
Side with painting: gold and color on silk, mounted
on paper; 12⅜ × 9⅛ in.
Francis Bartlett Donation of 1912 and Picture Fund,
14.545

PAGE 23: LUIS MELÉNDEZ
Italian (active in Spain), 1716–1780
Still Life with Bread, Ham, Cheese, and Vegetables, about 1770
Oil on canvas; 24⅜ × 33½ in.
Margaret Curry Wyman Fund, 39.40

PAGE 29: PIETER CLAESZ.
Dutch, 1597/1598–1661
Still Life with Wine Goblet and Oysters, 1630s
Oil on panel; 19¾ × 27⅝ in.
Gift of Mrs. H. P. Ahrnke in memory of her
great-aunt, Mrs. Francis B. Greene, 56.883

PAGE 31: WEI JIUDING
Chinese, active about 1350–1370
River Crab
Hanging scroll; ink on silk; 9¼ × 12½ in.
Keith McLeod Fund, 1996.244

PAGE 33: FRANS SNYDERS
Flemish, 1579–1657
Vegetables and a Basket of Fruit on a Table
Oil on canvas; 33 × 37¾ in.
Sidney Bartlett Bequest, 89.499

PAGE 34: Punch bowl and ladle
Rhode Island (Providence), about 1885
Manufactured by the Gorham Manufacturing
Company, active 1865–1961
Silver; punch bowl: 10⅛ × 15¾ in.
Edwin E. Jack Fund, 1980.383–384

PAGE 37: *The Luncheon* (from the series *La Noble Pastorale*
or *Les Beaux Pastorales*)
Tapestry
France (Beauvais), 1756
Tapestry weave; wool warp, wool and silk wefts;
137 × 133⅞ in.
Francis Bartlett Fund, 40.66

PAGE 39: *Three's Company*
Rhode Island (Providence), 1994
Made by Martin Simpson, American, born 1964
Maple, bleached wenge; 46 × 65½ × 21½ in.
Gift of The Seminarians, 1999.18
© Martin Simpson

PAGE 42: Soup tureen
England (Chelsea Factory), about 1755
Soft-paste porcelain with polychrome enamels;
10 × 15 in.
Jessie and Sigmund Katz Collection,
1972.1081a–b, 1972.1082

PAGE 47: PIERRE NICHON
French, active in 1645–1655
After Sebastian Stoskopff, born in Strasbourg,
about 1596–1657
Still Life with a Dead Carp on a Box
Oil on canvas; 19⅜ × 23¼ in.
Francis Welch Fund, 63.1628

PAGE 53: Bench
New Hampshire (Meriden), 1998
Made by Eric O'Leary, American, born 1949
Stoneware; 18 × 39⅝ × 14½ in.
Gift of Shin and Mako Abe, 1999.61
© Eric O'Leary

PAGE 55: UNIDENTIFIED ARTIST
American, mid-19th century
Tomatoes, Fruit, and Flowers, about 1860
Oil on canvas; 20 × 31½ in.
Gift of Martha C. Karolik for the M. and M. Karolik
Collection of American Paintings, 1815–1865, 47.1265

PAGE 56: Bowl
China, Qing dynasty, Kangxi period, early 18th century
Jingdezhen porcelain, enamel floral decoration;
height: 2½ in.
Gift of Paul and Helen Bernat, 1977.760

PAGE 59: Bed quilt
American, 1830s
Quilted white cotton with polychrome floral printed
appliqués; 116 × 114 in.
Gift of John M. Woolsey, 1992.246

PAGE 62: JOHN SINGLETON COPLEY
American, 1738–1815
Mrs. Ezekiel Goldthwait (Elizabeth Lewis), 1771
Oil on canvas; 50⅛ × 40⅛ in.
Bequest of John T. Bowen in memory of Eliza M.
Bowen, 41.84

PAGE 66: ROBERT RAUSCHENBERG
American, born 1925
Plain Salt (Cardboards), 1971
Cardboard and plywood; 80½ × 37 in.
Gift of Martin Peretz, 1992.396
© Robert Rauschenberg/Licensed by VAGA,
New York, NY

PAGE 69: Covered bowl and stand
France (Vincennes Factory), 1754
Ceramic; 6 × 8⅜ in.
Gift of Rita and Frits Markus of New York and
Chatham, Massachusetts, 1980.618a–c

PAGE 73: Settee
New York (Rochester), 1979
Made by Wendell Castle, American, born 1932
Cherry; 58 × 36 × 24 in.
The National Endowment for the Arts and the
Deborah M. Noonan Foundation, 1979.266
© Wendell Castle

PAGE 78: *Pueblo Bread Bakers*
New Mexico (Santa Clara Pueblo), 1984
Made by Joyce Sisneros, Native American, born 1944
Earthenware; 6¼ × 4¼ × 3½ in.
Gift of Dr. and Mrs. J. Wallace McMeel, 1984.775
© Joyce Sisneros

PAGE 83: HENRI MATISSE
French, 1869–1954
The Three Gourds, about 1916
Monotype; platemark: 5 × 7¹⁄₁₆ in.
Katherine E. Bullard Fund in memory of Francis
Bullard, 1990.245

PAGE 84: RUBENS PEALE
American, 1784–1865
Basket of Fruit, 1860
Oil on canvas; 14 × 22 in.
Bequest of Martha C. Karolik for the M. and M.
Karolik Collection of American Paintings, 1815–1865,
48.464

PAGE 86: JEROME B. THOMPSON
American, 1814–1886
A "Pic Nick," Camden, Maine, about 1850
Oil on canvas; 40⅞ × 62 in.
Gift of Maxim Karolik for the M. and M. Karolik
Collection of American Paintings, 1815–1865, 46.852

PAGE 89: Rocking chair
California (Alta Loma), 1975
Made by Sam Maloof, American, born 1916
Walnut; 45 × 27¾ × 46 in.
Purchased through funds provided by the National
Endowment for the Arts and the Gillette Corporation,
1976.122
© Sam Maloof

PAGE 91: Marsh bowl
Egypt, New Kingdom, Dynasty 18, 1539–1295/1292 B.C.
Faience; 1½ × 6³⁄₁₆ in.
William E. Nickerson Fund, 1977.619

PAGE 97: Skyphos (two-handled cup) with prepara-
tions for a Bacchic sacrifice
Roman, Imperial Period, A.D. 1–30
Silver with traces of gold leaf; height: 4⅜ in.
William Francis Warden Fund, Frank B. Bemis Fund,
John H. and Ernestine A. Payne Fund and William E.
Nickerson Fund, 1997.83

PAGE 98: Mushrooms netsuke
Japan, early to mid-19th century
Stained and polished boxwood; height: 1¹³⁄₁₆ in.
Gift of Dr. Ernest Goodrich Stillman, 47.474

PAGE 102: Lute (tambura)
India, 19th century
Gourd, jackwood; 53⅛ × 15¹⁵⁄₁₆ in.
Mary L. Smith Fund, 1992.259

PAGE 105: THOMAS ROWLANDSON
English, 1756–1827
The Man of Taste, about 1807
Pen, ink, and watercolor over graphite pencil; sheet:
9⁷⁄₁₆ × 13¹³⁄₁₆ in.
Gift of John T. Spaulding, 48.98

PAGE 108: Container in shape of mandarin duck
Vietnam, Le dynasty, late 15th century
Stoneware with underglaze blue decorations;
5½ × 9½ in.
Asiatic Curator's Fund, 1992.201

PAGE 113: Vessel in the form of a hare
Near Eastern, Syrian, Neolithic Period, about
6400–5900 B.C.
Gypsum; length: 7¼ in.
Egyptian Curator's Fund and Partial Gift of
Emmanuel Tiliakos, 1995.739

PAGE 115: KAIGETSUDO ANDO
Japanese, 1671–1743
Watermelon Slicer (detail), among miscellaneous genre
subjects
Handscroll; ink, color, gold, silver, and lacquer on
paper; 11⅛ × 260³⁄₁₆ in.
William Sturgis Bigelow Collection, 11.7498

PAGE 117: Wine cup
China, Qing dynasty, Kangxi period, early 18th century
Jingdezhen porcelain with overglaze enamel decoration
of plum blossoms; height: 1¹³⁄₁₆ in.
Gift of Paul and Helen Bernat, 60.1314

PAGE 118: HENRY SARGENT
American, 1770–1845
The Dinner Party, about 1821
Oil on canvas; 61⅝ × 49¾ in.
Gift of Mrs. Horatio A. Lamb in memory of Mr. and
Mrs. Winthrop Sargent, 19.13

Page 121: Side chairs
Massachusetts (Charlestown), 1987
Made by Peter Dean, American, born 1951
Pearwood, purpleheart, and lacquer; 43 × 20 × 19 in.
Gift of Anne and Ronald Abramson, 1987.461–462
© Peter Dean

PAGE 128: Ewer
Iran, Ilkhanid, about 1220–30
Beaten brass inlaid with silver; applied silver repoussé
details; height: 16⁷⁄₁₆ in.
Holmes Collection, 49.1901

PAGE 133: Side chair
Massachusetts (Northampton), 1989
Made by Kristina Madsen, American, born 1955
Pau ferro and maple; 36¾ × 19 × 17 in.
Gift of The Seminarians in honor of Jonathan L.
Fairbanks, 1991.452
© Kristina Madsen

PAGE 135: Ribbed bowl
Roman, Imperial Period, late 1st century B.C. to
1st century A.D.
Mosaic glass; height: 1¾ in.
Henry Lillie Pierce Fund, 99.442

PAGE 137: EDWARD WESTON
American, 1886–1958
Pepper, 1930
Photograph; gelatin silver print; 9½ × 7⁹⁄₁₆ in.
The Lane Collection

PAGE 140: Kalyx-krater (mixing bowl) with Dionysos,
a satyr, and a maenad
Greek, South Italian, Late Classical Period, about
345–335 B.C.
Italy, Apulia; close to Hippolyte Painter
Ceramic, Red figure; height: 16⅛ in.
Gift of Edythe K. Shulman, 1985.897

PAGE 148: JAMES PEALE
American, 1749–1831
A Porcelain Bowl with Fruit, 1830
Oil on canvas; 16⅜ × 22⅜ in.
Gift of JoAnn and Julian Ganz, Jr. and Emily L.
Ainsley Fund and Eliza Oliver Fund, 1979.520

PAGE 151: LEVI WELLS PRENTICE
American, 1851–1935
Apples in a Tin Pail, 1892
Oil on canvas; 16¼ × 13¼ in.
The Hayden Collection. Charles Henry Hayden Fund,
1978.468

PAGE 155: YOSHIDA HIROSHI
Japanese, 1876–1950
Greengrocer, Nezu, Japan, 1926
Woodblock print; ink and colors on paper,
16⁷⁄₁₆ × 10⅞ in.
Gift of L. Aaron Lebowich, 52.1452

PAGE 157: Chair
Massachusetts (Charlestown), 1985
Made by Jay Stanger, American, born 1956
Purpleheart, pau amarillo, anodized aluminum,
hard-coated red, blue, silver aluminum, cast epoxy;
51¼ × 19⅜ × 21 in.
Gift of Anne and Ronald Abramson, 1985.732
© Jay Stanger

PAGE 159: *Soleggiata Serena*
Rhode Island (Providence), 2000
Made by Toots Zynsky, American, born 1951
Fillet-de-verre glass; 11 × 24¾ × 9 in.
Gift of the artist in honor of Evelyn and John Zynsky,
2001.281
© Toots Zynsky

PAGE 162: UNIDENTIFIED ARTIST
American, mid-19th century
Egg Salad, about 1850
Oil on canvas; 8½ × 11¼ in.
Gift of Martha C. Karolik for the M. and M. Karolik
Collection of American Paintings, 1815–1865, 47.1220

PAGE 167: LU ZONGGUI
Chinese, Southern Song dynasty, 13th century
Orange, Grapes and Pomegranates Square Album Leaf
Ink and color on silk; 9⁷⁄₁₆ × 10³⁄₁₆ in.
Charles Bain Hoyt Collection, 50.1454

PAGE 172: Cylinder vase
Maya, Mexico (Campeche), A.D. 600–750
Earthenware: red, white, and black slip paint on
yellow-cream slip ground; 7⅞ × 6¹¹⁄₁₆ in.
Gift of Landon T. Clay, 1988.1169

PAGE 174: Grand piano
England (London), 1796
Manufactured by John Broadwood & Son
Satinwood, purpleheart, tulipwood; medallions by
Josiah Wedgwood; coin casts by James Tassie; case
designed by Thomas Sheraton; 97⅞ × 43⅞ × 35⅞ in.
The George Alfred Cluett Collection, given by
Florence Cluett Chambers, 1985.924

PAGE 177: Stela of Ahmose
Egypt, New Kingdom, Dynasty 18, 1539–1292 B.C.
Painted limestone; 19½ × 11⅝ in.
Egyptian Special Purchase Fund, 1981.2

PAGE 178: Evening ensemble
France (Paris), winter collection 1935–36
Designed by Jeanne Lavin, French, 1867–1946
Silk crepe, trimmed in gilded leather
Gift of Miss Lucy T. Aldrich, 51.2627a–b

PAGE 180: *Glacier Bench*
California (Oakland), 1997
Made by John Lewis, American, born 1942
Cast glass; 19 × 60 × 18 in.
Museum purchase, 1997.952
© John Lewis

Acknowledgments

The Ladies Committee (recently renamed MFA Associates) was founded in 1956 to promote and enhance membership in the Museum of Fine Arts, Boston. It strives to make the Museum a positive and enriching experience for all visitors. The seventy members, who serve four-year terms, represent many geographical and cultural communities.

An outgrowth of the Ladies Committee, the Ladies Committee Associates (now MFA Senior Associates) was established in 1965 to provide an opportunity for continued interest and service to the Museum. Membership, which is open to all who have served a minimum of two years on the Ladies Committee, currently numbers more than four hundred.

Both organizations collaborated in the creation of four very successful but now out-of-print cookbooks illustrated with works of art from the permanent collection of the Museum. In 2000, with underwriting help from the Ladies Committee, the Cookbook Committee members revised and updated the popular 1987 *Boston Tea Parties.* This volume, *Please Be Seated,* continues the commitment of the organization to publish outstanding recipes in this millennium.

COOKBOOK COMMITTEE

Molly Batchelder	Kim Hublitz	Ann Schwarz
Judith Chamberlain	Phyllis Katz	Joanne Seiden
Betsy Heald	Nancy McMahon	Kathryn Thomas

The committee wishes to thank the members of the MFA Associates, the MFA Senior Associates, Museum staff, and friends who generously shared their favorite recipes. More than three hundred recipes were submitted by the Museum community, evaluated by the Cookbook Committee, and tested by dedicated MFA Senior Associate cooking enthusiasts. In some instances, recipes were altered by the committee, or they served as the inspiration for other recipes.

COOKBOOK TESTERS

Anne Becklean
Louise Berry
Carol Casey
Cynthia Chapman
Monique Clute
Ellen Fallon
Jean Ferguson
JoAnn Haynes
Sylvia Hutter
Marta Johnston
Barbara Leith
Marybel Lucas
Marilyn MacLellan
Betsy McMeel
Mike Mechem
Libby Mottur
Evelyn Umlas
Rose-Marie van Otterloo
Cookbook Committee

RECIPE CONTRIBUTORS

Barbara Alfond
Corrine Allard
Terry Aufranc
Marilyn Ayer
Pamela J. Bakos
Molly Batchelder
Carl Beck
Anne Becklean
Louise Berry
Ann Blanchard
Carol Casey
Carolyn Y. Cate
Benjamin Cevelo
Judith Chamberlain
Jo Cleary
Ann Cogswell
Frannie Colburn
Caroline E. Cornish
Nancy DeLong
Patty Dooley
Mary Dunlap
Nancy Eskandarian
Susan Fesus
Lulie Finlay
Helen Fraser
Martha Fritz
Betty Georgaklis
Todd Gilman
Eleanor Glimp
Ed Gonski
Genevieve Good
Jean Gottesman
Judy Gray
Phyllis Gray

Anne Harper
Betsy Heald
Pamela S. Henrikson
Jane Hinkley
Marti Hood
Anne Howard
Kim Hublitz
Rosemary Hudson
Dolph Hutter
Sylvia Hutter
Sandy Janes
Marta Johnston
Susan Johnston
Phyllis Katz
Wendy W. Keleher
Bernard Kelly
Janet Sears Kostoff
Ginny Ladd
Linda Ladd
Julie Lapham
Frances W. Lawrence
Katharine Lawrence
Marilyn MacLellan
Peter Major
Rae Ann Mandell
Darcy Marsh
Judy Marshall
Dorothy D. Martin
Nancy McMahon
Betsy McMeel
Catherine L. Medaglia
Diane Miller
Aaron Miranda
Libby Mottur

Roy Perkinson

Jo Plank

Grace Polizzotti

Ruth Potter

Polly Pyne

Sue Reed

Meg Robbins

Mary Roetzel

Anne Rogers

Christine Root

Patty Russell

Gerry Scheide

Shirley Schlothauer

Ann Schwarz

Joanne Seiden

Marilyn Myers Slade

Ruth Smith

Gloria Sonnabend

Allys Spilios

Jacquie Stepanian

Ellen Stillman

Patricia Storey

Doris Sullivan

Jean S. Szen

Severn Taylor

Kathryn Thomas

Marcia Thomas

Jeanne Towles

Evelyn Umlas

Pege Verani

Anne Vernon

Natalie L. Webster

Katharine White

Abigail Winans

In addition, the committee is grateful to Cookbook Committee Treasurer Carolyn Marsh, Ladies Committee Associates Chairmen Marilyn MacLellan and Susie Cogan, Ladies Committee Chairmen Terry Aufranc and Barbara Alfond, and the Ladies Committee and Ladies Committee Associates for their unflagging support and promotion of this project.

Especially helpful to the committee were Director of Publications Mark Polizzotti as well as the following MFA staff members: Christopher Atkins, Tom Lang, Julia McCarthy, Angela Segalla, and Pat Warner. Sincere thanks to them, to former Membership staff Carl Beck and Charles Thomas, and to other members of the Museum staff for their expert advice and assistance: Clifford S. Ackley, Brenda Breed, Cheryl Brutvan, Elizabeth Ann Coleman, Joan Cummins, Amy Dalton, Erika Field, Rita Freed, Joseph Gajda, Sachi Govindan, Karen Haas, Sean Halpert, John Hermann, Lisa Krassner, Darcy Kuronen, Deborah LaKind, Cecelia Levin, Peter Matthews, Dennis McGrath, Stephanie Miller, William O'Connor, Marianne Pitkin, Karen Quinn, Jennifer Riley, George Shackelford, Kaitlin Shinnick, Angie Simonds, Kevin Sparrow, Stephanie Stepanek, Julia Valiela, Gerald Ward, and Wu Tung.

And finally, our appreciation, too, to Saundra Lane for permission to use the Edward Weston photograph from her private collection.

Index

Apple Cheese Torte, 167

Apple Peach Crumble, 166

Apricot Onion Chutney, 150

Artichoke Cheesecake, 21

Asian Pork Tenderloin, 115

Asian Stuffed Portobello Mushrooms, 99

Asparagus Linguine with Herb Brown Butter, 127

Baked Indian Pudding, 165

Baked Rotini with Sausage and Feta, 129

Baked Scrod with Crumb Topping, 93

Baked Semolina Gnocchi, 145

Beet Salad with Walnuts and Baked Goat Cheese, 60

BEVERAGES, 34

    Egg Nog, 36

    Fire Punch, 36

    Holiday Hot Mulled Punch, 35

    London Mimosa, 35

    Passion Fruit Punch, 35

    Rhubarb Punch, 34

Big Dig Mud, 177

Black Bean Salad, 58

Blueberry Buckle, 82

Bluefish with Mustard, 90

Boston Baked Beans, 146

Boston Brown Bread, 74

Boston Cream Pie, 178

Bread Crumbs, Fresh, 144

BREADS, 74

    Boston Brown Bread, 74

    Dill Bread, 79

    Irish Soda Bread, 76

    Shredded Wheat Bread, 78

    Sun-dried Tomato Herb Bread, 75

    Walnut Onion Bread, 75

Butterflied Leg of Lamb, 101

Cape Cod Bluefish, 91

Caramelized Onion Quesadillas, 30

CASSEROLES, 122

    Moussaka, 122

    Risotto with Spicy Sausage and Mushrooms, 124

    Smoked Salmon and Spinach Risotto, 125

    West Indian Curry, 123

Celestial Crème, 163

Cherry Clafouti, 169

Chicken Chutney Canapés, 23

Chicken Liver Pâté, 24

Chicken and Two Rice Salad, 64

Chiles and Cheese, 21

Chinese Baby Back Ribs, 117

Chinese Chili Shrimp, 93

Chocolate Supreme Mousse Cake Roll, 174

CHOWDERS, 49

    New England Seafood Chowder, 50

    Oven Fish Chowder, 49

    Sweet Potato Chowder, 51

Citrus Butter, 153

Citrus Salad, 63

Cold Senegalese Soup, 40

CONDIMENTS, 149

    Apricot Onion Chutney, 150

    Citrus Butter, 153

    Cranberry, Apple, and Pear Chutney, 150

    Curry, Accompaniments for, 152

    Miso Sauce, 153

    Mustard Sauce, 154

    New England Baked Cranberry Sauce, 149

    Pesto Genovese, 154

    Red Onion Marmalade, 152

    Teriyaki Sauce, 154

    Wasabi Butter, 153

Cornbread Stuffing, 144

Country Chicken, 97

Cranberry, Apple, and Pear Chutney, 150

Cranberry Carrot Salad, 61

Cream Kadayif, 164

Crème Fraîche, 68

Crown Roast of Pork, 116

Cucumber Horseradish Dressing, 68

Cumin Basmati Rice, 147

Curried Zucchini Soup, 41

Curry, Accompaniments for, 152

Curry Chutney Mayonnaise, 67

Curry Powder, 70

CUSTARDS, 162

    Baked Indian Pudding, 165

    Celestial Crème, 163

    Cream Kadayif, 164

    Lighter Custard Sauce, 162

    Maple Syrup Pudding Cake, 165

    Peach Velvet, 163

Dill Bread, 79
DRESSINGS, 67
    Crème Fraîche, 68
    Cucumber Horseradish Dressing, 68
    Curry Chutney Mayonnaise, 67
    One-Minute Blender Mayonnaise, 67
    Wasabi Mayonnaise, 68
Egg Nog, 36
Eggplant Crostini, 27
Eggplant with Parmesan Curls, 32
Eggplant "Sandwiches," 131
Elegant Crab Bisque, 45
Equipment, 17
Fallen Chocolate Soufflé Cake, 172
Field Greens, Roasted Tomatoes, and Jicama, 55
Fillet of Beef Tenderloin, 107
Fire Punch, 36
FIRST COURSES, 30
    Caramelized Onion Quesadillas, 30
    Eggplant with Parmesan Curls, 32
    Marinated Mussels, 30
    Salmon Crab Cakes, 31
French Spice Mix, 71
Fresh Blueberry Tart, 168
Fresh Fruit Brûlé, 161
Fresh Herb Sandwich, 87
Fruited Pilaf, 148
Fruited Pork Tenderloin, 114
FRUITS, 158
    Fresh Fruit Brûlé, 161
    Melon Balls with Lime Sauce, 158
    Melons in Sweet Wine, 158
    Oranges Aviz, 159
    Summer Pudding, 160
German Chicken, 98
GRAINS, 144
    Baked Semolina Gnocchi, 145
    Boston Baked Beans, 146
    Bread Crumbs, Fresh, 144
    Cornbread Stuffing, 144
    Cumin Basmati Rice, 147
    Fruited Pilaf, 148
    Wild Rice with Mushrooms, 147
Greek Peasant Salad, 60
Greek-Style Shrimp with Pasta, 126
Green Beans with Sesame Dressing, 58
Grilled Vegetable Gazpacho, 44
Hamburgers with Blue Cheese, 113
Hazelnut Cheesecake, 171
Hearty Fisherman's Stew, 48
Herb Salt, 70

Herbed Dumplings, 85
Holiday Hot Mulled Punch, 35
Horns, 81
HORS D'OEUVRES, 21
    Artichoke Cheesecake, 21
    Chicken Chutney Canapés, 23
    Chicken Liver Pâté, 24
    Chiles and Cheese, 21
    Eggplant Crostini, 27
    Marinated Mushrooms, 22
    Marinated Shrimp, 27
    Provençal Tartlets, 26
    Smoked Salmon Toasts, 24
    Spicy Mussels, 28
    Summer Shrimp Salsa, 25
    Sweet Pea Guacamole, 22
Ingredients, 11
Irish Soda Bread, 76
Japanese Grilled Beef, 109
Korean Broiled Beef, 108
Lamb Shanks with White Beans, 102
Lighter Custard Sauce, 162
Linguine with Seared Shrimp, 127
Lobster Salad, 65
London Mimosa, 35
Maple Smashed Sweet Potatoes, 141
Maple Syrup Pudding Cake, 165
Marinated Broccoli, 136
Marinated Chicken with Spicy Peanut Sauce, 96
Marinated Mushrooms, 22
Marinated Mussels, 30
Marinated Shrimp, 27
MEATS, 100
    Beef, 107
        Fillet of Beef Tenderloin, 107
        Hamburgers with Blue Cheese, 113
        Japanese Grilled Beef, 109
        Korean Broiled Beef, 108
        New England Boiled Dinner, 111
        Pinwheel Meatloaf, 112
        Yankee Pot Roast, 110
    Lamb, 100
        Butterflied Leg of Lamb, 101
        Lamb Shanks with White Beans, 102
        Mongolian Lamb, 100
    Pork, 114
        Asian Pork Tenderloin, 115
        Chinese Baby Back Ribs, 117
        Crown Roast of Pork, 116
        Fruited Pork Tenderloin, 114
        Stuffed Red Peppers, 119

Veal, 104
    Veal Creole, 106
    Veal Scaloppine with Peppers, 104
    Veal Zurich Style, 105
Mediterranean Stuffed Chicken Breasts, 95
Melon Balls with Lime Sauce, 158
Melons in Sweet Wine, 158
Mesclun Greens with Goat Cheese and Candied
   Walnuts, 54
Mesclun Greens with Pine Nuts, 54
Methods, 15
Microwave Szechuan Green Beans, 138
Mint-Marinated Grilled Red Onions, 135
Miso Sauce, 153
Mongolian Lamb, 100
Moussaka, 122
Mustard Sauce, 154
New England Baked Cranberry Sauce, 149
New England Boiled Dinner, 111
New England Seafood Chowder, 50
Norwegian Spiced Cookies, 169
"One of Each" Soup, 40
One-Minute Blender Mayonnaise, 67
Oranges Aviz, 159
Orecchiette with Broccoflower, 128
Oven Fish Chowder, 49
Panzanella, 57
Parker House Rolls, 80
Passion Fruit Punch, 35
PASTAS, 126
    Asparagus Linguine with Herb Brown Butter, 127
    Baked Rotini with Sausage and Feta, 129
    Greek-Style Shrimp with Pasta, 126
    Linguine with Seared Shrimp, 127
    Orecchiette with Broccoflower, 128
Peach Pie Surprise, 168
Peach Velvet, 163
Pear and Leek Bisque, 43
Pesto Genovese, 154
Pinwheel Meatloaf, 112
Popovers, 84
Potato Pancakes with Scallions and Prosciutto, 143
Potato Puff, 143
POULTRY, 95
    Asian Stuffed Portobello Mushrooms, 99
    Country Chicken, 97
    German Chicken, 98
    Marinated Chicken with Spicy Peanut Sauce, 96
    Mediterranean Stuffed Chicken Breasts, 95
Pound Cake, 176
Provençal Tartlets, 26

Pumpkin Pancakes, 82
QUICHES, 130
    Eggplant "Sandwiches," 131
    Savory Cheese Tart, 130
    Smoked Salmon and Dill Quesadilla, 131
    Soufflé Sandwich with Crabmeat, 130
Red Bliss Potato Salad with Vinaigrette, 141
Red Onion Marmalade, 152
Rhubarb Punch, 34
Risotto with Spicy Sausage and Mushrooms, 124
Roast Bass with Caramelized Onions, 94
Roasted Asparagus, 136
Roasted Bell Peppers with Walnuts, 137
Roasted Caramelized Onions, 135
ROLLS, 80
    Blueberry Buckle, 82
    Herbed Dumplings, 85
    Horns, 81
    Parker House Rolls, 80
    Popovers, 84
    Pumpkin Pancakes, 82
    Savory Madeleines, 85
    Tea Ring, 81
SALADS, 54
    Beet Salad with Walnuts and Baked Goat Cheese, 60
    Black Bean Salad, 58
    Chicken and Two Rice Salad, 64
    Citrus Salad, 63
    Cranberry Carrot Salad, 61
    Field Greens, Roasted Tomatoes, and Jicama, 55
    Green Beans with Sesame Dressing, 58
    Greek Peasant Salad, 60
    Lobster Salad, 65
    Mesclun Greens with Goat Cheese and Candied
      Walnuts, 54
    Mesclun Greens with Pine Nuts, 54
    Panzanella, 57
    Solar Summer Salad, 63
    Summer Salad, 61
Salmon Crab Cakes, 31
SANDWICHES, 87
    Fresh Herb Sandwich, 87
    Hamburgers with Blue Cheese, 113
    Versatile Vegetarian Sandwich, 87
Savory Cheese Tart, 130
Savory Madeleines, 85
Scallops in Wine, 92
SEAFOOD, 90
    Baked Scrod with Crumb Topping, 93
    Bluefish with Mustard, 90
    Cape Cod Bluefish, 91

SEAFOOD (*cont.*)
 Chinese Chili Shrimp, 93
 Roast Bass with Caramelized Onions, 94
 Scallops in Wine, 92
 Steamed Mussels with Pancetta, 92
 Swordfish Nantucket, 90
SEASONINGS, 70
 Curry Powder, 70
 French Spice Mix, 71
 Herb Salt, 70
Shredded Wheat Bread, 78
Shrimp Soup, 45
Simple Seafood Stew, 46
Skillet Tomatoes, 138
Smoked Salmon and Dill Quesadilla, 131
Smoked Salmon and Spinach Risotto, 125
Smoked Salmon Toasts, 24
Solar Summer Salad, 63
Soufflé Sandwich with Crabmeat, 130
SOUPS, 40
 Cold Senegalese Soup, 40
 Curried Zucchini Soup, 41
 Elegant Crab Bisque, 45
 Grilled Vegetable Gazpacho, 44
 "One of Each" Soup, 40
 Pear and Leek Bisque, 43
 Shrimp Soup, 45
 White Gazpacho, 43
 Wild Rice Soup, 41
Spicy Mussels, 28
Spinach Cabrini, 134
Steamed Mussels with Pancetta, 92
STEWS, 46
 Hearty Fisherman's Stew, 48
 Simple Seafood Stew, 46
Stuffed Red Peppers, 119
Succotash with a Dash, 139
Summer Pudding, 160
Summer Salad, 61
Summer Shrimp Salsa, 25
Sun-dried Tomato Herb Bread, 75
Sweet Pea Guacamole, 22
Sweet Potato Chowder, 51
Sweet Potato Pie, 142
SWEETS, 166
 Apple Cheese Torte, 167
 Apple Peach Crumble, 166
 Big Dig Mud, 177
 Boston Cream Pie, 178
 Cherry Clafouti, 169
 Chocolate Supreme Mousse Cake Roll, 174
 Fallen Chocolate Soufflé Cake, 172
 Fresh Blueberry Tart, 168
 Hazelnut Cheesecake, 171
 Norwegian Spiced Cookies, 169
 Peach Pie Surprise, 168
 Pound Cake, 175
 Swiss Meringue Tart, 170
Swiss Meringue Tart, 170
Swordfish Nantucket, 90
Tea Ring, 81
Teriyaki Sauce, 154
Veal Creole, 106
Veal Scaloppine with Peppers, 104
Veal Zurich Style, 105
VEGETABLES, 134
 Maple Smashed Sweet Potatoes, 141
 Marinated Broccoli, 136
 Microwave Szechuan Green Beans, 138
 Mint-Marinated Grilled Red Onions, 134
 Potato Pancakes with Scallions and Prosciutto, 143
 Potato Puff, 143
 Red Bliss Potato Salad with Vinaigrette, 141
 Roasted Asparagus, 136
 Roasted Bell Peppers with Walnuts, 137
 Roasted Caramelized Onions, 135
 Skillet Tomatoes, 138
 Spinach Cabrini, 134
 Succotash with a Dash, 139
 Sweet Potato Pie, 142
Versatile Vegetarian Sandwich, 87
Walnut Onion Bread, 75
Wasabi Butter, 153
Wasabi Mayonnaise, 68
West Indian Curry, 123
White Gazpacho, 43
Wild Rice with Mushrooms, 147
Wild Rice Soup, 41
Yankee Pot Roast, 110
Yeast Bread Hints, 77